T0383837

Timeless Leadership Truths: The Origins and Applications of Business Strategy

Timeless Leadership Truths: The Origins and Applications of Business Strategy

Norton Paley

Routledge
Taylor & Francis Group

A PRODUCTIVITY PRESS BOOK

First edition published in 2020
by Routledge/Productivity Press
52 Vanderbilt Avenue, 11th Floor New York, NY 10017
2 Park Square, Milton Park, Abingdon, Oxon OX14 4RN, UK

International Standard Book Number-13: 978-0-367-32155-0 (Hardback)
International Standard Book Number-13: 978-0-429-31716-3 (eBook)

Library of Congress Cataloging-in-Publication Data

Names: Paley, Norton, author.
Title: Timeless leadership truths : the origins and applications of business strategy / Norton Paley.
Description: 1 Edition. | New York : Routledge, [2020]
Identifiers: LCCN 2019014904 (print) | LCCN 2019015512 (ebook) | ISBN 9780429317163 (e-Book) | ISBN 9780367321550 (hardback : alk. paper)
Subjects: LCSH: Business planning. | Leadership.
Classification: LCC HD30.28 (ebook) | LCC HD30.28 .P2854 2020 (print) | DDC 658.4/012--dc23
LC record available at https://lccn.loc.gov/2019014904

Visit the Taylor & Francis Web site at
http://www.taylorandfrancis.com

Visit the Routledge/Productivity Web site at
https://www.routledge.com/

In loving memory of Hubert Paley:

Brother, friend, artist, mensch.

Contents

APPLICATIONS

PART 3   Activating a Business Strategy: Developing a Strategic Business Plan

PART 4   Origins and Applications of the Digital-Age Organization

About the Author

Norton Paley has brought his world-class experience and unique approach to business strategy to some of the global community's most respected organizations.

Having launched his career with publishing giants McGraw-Hill and John Wiley & Sons, Paley founded Alexander-Norton Inc., bringing successful business techniques to clients around the globe including the international training organization Strategic Management Group, where he served as senior consultant.

Throughout his career, Paley has trained business managers and their staff in the areas of planning and strategy development, raising the bar for achievement and forging new approaches to problem solving and competitive edge.

His clients include:

- American Express
- IBM
- Detroit Edison
- Chrysler (Parts Division)
- McDonnell-Douglas
- Dow Chemical (Worldwide)
- W. R. Grace
- Cargill (Worldwide)
- Chevron Chemical
- Ralston-Purina
- Johnson & Johnson
- Celanese
- Hoechst
- Mississippi Power
- Numerous mid-sized and small firms

Paley has lectured in the Republic of China and Mexico and he has presented training seminars throughout the Pacific Rim and Europe for Dow Chemical and Cargill.

As a seminar leader at the American Management Association, he conducted competitive strategy, marketing management, and strategic planning programs for over 20 years.

Published books include:

- *Effective Leadership Strategies for the Digital Age*
- *Leadership Strategies in the Age of Big Data, Algorithms, and Analytics*
- *Developing a Turnaround Business Plan: Leadership Techniques to Achieve Change Strategies, Secure Competitive Advantage, and Preserve Success*
- *Clausewitz Talks Business: An Executive's Guide to Thinking Like a Strategist*
- *How to Outthink, Outmaneuver and Outperform Your Competitors: Lessons from the Masters of Strategy*
- *Mastering the Rules of Competitive Strategy: A Resource Guide for Managers*
- *The Marketing Strategy Desktop Guide, 2nd Edition*
- *How to Develop A Strategic Marketing Plan**
- *The Managers Guide to Competitive Marketing Strategies, 3rd Edition*
- *Marketing for the Nonmarketing Executive: An Integrated Management Resource Guide for the 21st Century*
- *Successful Business Planning: Energizing Your Company's Potential*
- *Manage to Win*†
- *Big Ideas for Small Businesses*

On the cusp of the interactive movement, Paley developed three computer-based, interactive training systems: *The Marketing Learning Systems*; *Segmentation, Targeting & Positioning*; and *The Marketing Planning System*.

Paley's books have been translated into Chinese, Russian, Portuguese, and Turkish.

His byline columns have appeared in *The Management Review* and *Sales & Marketing Management* magazines.

---

* "This book is both intellectual and practical … an interesting vehicle for presenting detailed planning concepts … it is clear and well-organized." T. J. Belich, in *CHOICE*. Also selected for translation into Chinese and Turkish.

† "A book too forceful to ignore." Review in *Business Line, Financial Daily* for The Hindu Group of Publications.

Introduction

Although separated in time by about 2,300 years and further divided by experiences, geography, history, politics, and cultures, these two statements are remarkably similar in terms of how both generals viewed conflict.

In other writings, Clausewitz went on to say, "we could more accurately compare conflict to commerce, which is also a conflict of human interests and activities."

And Sun Tzu counseled, "supreme excellence consists in breaking the enemy's resistance without fighting."

Why, then, look to the origins of business strategy in military applications? And what is its relationship to managing a business where conflict is easily compared to competitive struggles?

Generals throughout the ages faced formidable challenges as they crafted plans to outmaneuver competing forces, acquire territory, and gain power. Similarly, business leaders also looked to outmaneuver their rivals as they entered new markets against entrenched competitors, secured a strong market position, and expanded their companies' influence.

Consider, too, the conflicts among the following organizations that persist in ongoing battles:

Coke vs. Pepsi, Nike vs. Reebok, Microsoft vs. Apple, CVS vs. Walgreens, UPS vs. FedEx, Google vs. Facebook, BMW vs. Lexus, Visa vs. MasterCard, Airbus vs. Boeing, P&G vs. Unilever, Bayer vs. Tylenol. And the list remains combative in virtually every marketplace.

Although the destructive aspects of war are not present in business, there is a reasonable parallel. Think of the bankruptcy of once-mighty Eastman Kodak or the reorganization of the iconic General Electric; both incidents resulted in layoffs of thousands of employees and the closings of numerous plants.

Then, there was the devastating economic impact and societal disruption that created demoralizing misery among large groups of individuals in once-flourishing cities, such as Detroit, Michigan, as well as numerous other once-thriving areas worldwide.

Beginning in the 1960s, many business scholars, leaders, and line managers started to accept the military–business connection. They found practical wisdom in studying both Sun Tzu and Clausewitz. And by examining the strategic and human elements of clashes that span recorded history, they gained valuable insights, which provided a new level of thinking about business and competitive strategy.

One of those individuals was Bruce Henderson of the Boston Consulting Group, who dealt with issues of strategy by relating them to their military roots. Henderson especially valued the military emphasis on maneuvering through the indirect approach and concentrating strength against a rival's weaknesses.

He also sensed the drama of competition and discussed the trickery that might be employed to divert competitors. The lessons of strategy, he thought, could be applied to differences in leadership style, as well as to matters of overhead rate, distribution channels, or corporate image.

Noted business scholar Professor Philip Kotler also examined the military–business connection in the article "Marketing Warfare in the 1980s." With co-author Ravi Singh, he argued that "to develop competitor-centered strategies to win market share will lead managers to turn increasingly to the subject of military science."

Then, in 1986, Jack Trout and Al Ries wrote the highly popular *Marketing Warfare*, which referenced Clausewitz. The authors focused on the psychological aspects of occupying the mind of the consumer, rather than territory. And just like the strongest armies, the strongest companies should be able to use their power to stay on top.

As for small companies, to have a fighting chance, like small armies, they must employ cunning rather than brute force against a large organization in a well-entrenched defensive position. Altogether, Trout and Ries became well known for their applications of four military-centered strategies: *defensive, offensive, flanking,* and *guerrilla.*

Consider, too, the everyday language of business. It is common to read in the business press, or hear at seminars and workshops, the combative vocabulary borrowed from the military with such phrases as *attacking a competitor, developing a strong position, defending a market, strengthening logistics, deploying personnel, launching a campaign, developing a strategy, outflanking rivals, utilizing tactics, coping with price wars, doing battle with* ... and other familiar comments.

Also, there are more indirect references that connect military to business, such as *holding reserves to exploit a market advantage, developing an intelligence network to track a competitor's actions, avoiding direct confrontation with the market leader, bypassing a market because of high entry barriers, reorganizing the marketing and sales effort to strengthen a market position,* or *employing a new technology to create a competitive advantage over a weaker rival.*

ORIGINS

The modern-day use of *strategy* is traced to the ancient Greek words *strategia* or *strategike.* These terms mean the art of the commander or generalship. In 1777, a German translation used the term *strategie,* which evolved into the English *strategy.*

Many writers have contributed valuable doctrines to form the body of knowledge that further defined strategy. These include such ancient writers as Thucydides, Polybius, and Plutarch. Then, there were other notable writers, such as Vegetius, Machiavelli, and Jomini.

Yet none of their works gained the world-wide acclaim and long-lasting notoriety of Sun Tzu and Carl von Clausewitz. It is the incomparable writings of these two that are featured in this book.

Their concepts remain current and give authority to the workings of a business in a competitive environment, which is attributed to two main factors.

> First, the underlying patterns of human nature have not changed significantly throughout history.
>
> Second, notwithstanding the geographical, political, and technological changes, the pragmatic logic supporting strategy retains its value today as it has since the appearance of Sun Tzu's *The Art of War* over 2,000 years ago and Clausewitz's *On War* from the 19th century.

Some fields, particularly those in science, medicine, technology, and economics, are continually updated in response to breakthrough discoveries. In contrast, many of the historic treatises in the humanities remain as noteworthy and valuable as the day they were written.

It is the study of warfare, however, that fits a special category. Fighting, combat, feud, rivalry, competition, and power struggles give a human face to conflict. Thus, by focusing on the distinguishing qualities of human behavior, leadership, and organizational culture, you can benefit from a broader perspective that leads to a better understanding of your business problems. In turn, you hone the skills to apply appropriate strategies to outmaneuver competitive obstacles.

Yet in all the foregoing discussion, fighting may appear to be the object of warfare, and aggressive business competition may appear to be the endgame. From Sun Tzu's opening statement, just the opposite is true, as he further states:

> *Know the enemy and know yourself; in a hundred battles you will never be in peril.*
>
> *When you are ignorant of the enemy but know yourself, your chances of winning or losing are equal.*
>
> *If ignorant both of your enemy and of yourself, you are certain in every battle to be in peril.*

And from Clausewitz:

> *In conflict even the ultimate outcome is never to be regarded as final. The outcome is merely a transitory evil, for which a remedy may still be found in a variety of possible conditions at some later date.*
>
> *A leader must never expect to move on the narrow ground of imagined security and feel that the means he is using are the only ones possible—and persist in using them even at the thought of their possible inadequacy.*

The intent of this book, therefore, is to heighten the level of your strategic thinking. The further aim is to blend Sun Tzu's and Clausewitz's timeless truths into your business plans and strategies so as to impact on grass-roots encounters with customers and the inevitable clashes with competitors.*

As importantly, you will benefit from a body of knowledge that has endured in written form and has been practiced by successful leaders for centuries. Doing so permits you to think like a strategist, which will give you the edge in an evolving digital-age competitive marketplace.

Finally, scholars, historians, consultants, and others provide numerous definitions of *strategy*. The one used in this book is the following:

Strategy is the art of coordinating the means (money, human resources, and materials) to achieve the ends (profit, customer satisfaction, and company growth) as defined by the organization's vision, policies, and objectives.

A more direct and pragmatic definition is that strategies are actions to achieve your longer-term objectives; tactics are actions to achieve shorter-term objectives.

---

* To gain the most from Sun Tzu's and Clausewitz's wisdom, I have made every effort to retain the essence of their writings. The only change I have made is to substitute their war jargon with familiar business vocabulary, such as *rival* for *enemy*, *resources* or *technologies* for *weapons*, and the like.

Origins

Origins

Part 1

Sun Tzu

OVERVIEW

B. H. Liddell Hart*

Sun Tzu's essays on The Art of War form the earliest of known treatises on the subject but have never been surpassed in comprehensiveness and depth of understanding. They might well be termed the concentrated essence of wisdom on the conduct of war.

For over 2,500 years, Sun Tzu's wisdom and clarity of thought have endured. Individuals from all walks of life have interpreted his famous 13 chapters and extracted fresh insights from his profound doctrines.

---

* Sir B. H. Liddell Hart (1895–1970) was an English soldier, military historian, and author. He is best known for his concept of the indirect strategy, which he viewed as a valid strategy in other fields of endeavor, such as business and sports.

It is thought that Napoleon read the book when it was published in Paris in 1782. And it is likely that two great military theorists, Carl von Clausewitz and Antoine-Henri de Jomini, were familiar with Sun Tzu.

Sun Tzu's inspiration carried into the twentieth century and influenced such military giants as British field marshal Bernard Montgomery, US generals Douglas MacArthur and George Patton, and German general Heinz Guderian. Mao Zedong and Fidel Castro also embraced Sun Tzu's theories.

Worth noting, too, is how far afield Sun Tzu has reached from the military. In the movie *Wall Street*, the character Gordon Gekko says, "I bet on sure things. Read Sun Tzu, The Art of War. Every battle is won before it is ever fought." Then, in the popular television series, *The Sopranos*, Tony Soprano remarked, "Been reading that book … The Art of War by Sun Tzu. A Chinese general wrote this thing 2,400 years ago, and most of it still applies today."

Who was Sun Tzu?

He was born in a region of China known today as Huiming County, Shandong Province. However, there is no accurate record of Sun Tzu's actual dates of birth and death. Scholars have conflicting theories about the authorship of the book—if it was written by one person or was a compilation of other authors' writings.

The generally accepted view is that one individual wrote it, Sun Tzu. The "Tzu" in his name means "master," or Master Sun, whereas his personal name is Sun Wu. In the famous 1910 translation of *The Art of War*, Lionel Giles stated that the work would have been written between 496 BCE and 494 BCE.

To this day, Sun Tzu's *The Art of War* endures. His profound wisdom continues to survive meticulous analysis by scholars and practitioners. Translated into numerous languages worldwide, the book is incorporated into the curricula at universities and military academies. And his time-tested ideas, concepts, and rules continue to flourish today in business books, magazines, and workshops.

The following is a sampling of Sun Tzu's concepts from the following chapters:

There is no instance of a country having benefited from prolonged warfare.

Tactics are like unto water; for water in its natural course runs away from high places and hastens downward. So, in war, the way to avoid what is strong is to strike what is weak.

Rapidity is the essence of war; take advantage of the enemy's unreadiness, make your way by unexpected routes and attack unguarded spots.

Know the enemy and know yourself, in a hundred battles you will never be in peril.
   When you are ignorant of the enemy but know yourself, your chances of winning or losing are equal.
   If ignorant of both your enemy and yourself, you are certain in every battle to be in peril.

All men can see the tactics by which I do battle, but none can see the strategy by which I win victory.

In all fighting, the direct method may be used for joining battle, but indirect methods will be needed to secure victory.

1

Prosperity, Survival, or Ruin

Sun Tzu

Performing in a competitive marketplace is a matter of vital importance to the organization; the province of prosperity; the road to survival or ruin. Study it thoroughly.*

APPLICATIONS

Sun Tzu's comment about "the road to survival or ruin" is relevant when viewed through the shocking decline of once majestic organizations, such as the 2018 bankruptcy of Sears. Consider, too, the demise of once vibrant communities and its economic toll on families and individuals' careers.

And "study it thoroughly" takes on special meaning when a company is faced with any of the following types of market campaigns, where scarce resources are at risk:

- Campaigns to introduce a new product where on average 50% of new product launches fail.†
- Offensive campaigns to recover a former market position.

---

* For clarity, I have recast Sun Tzu's statements in modern business vocabulary, while maintaining the essential meaning of his counsel. For instance, the original translation reads, "War is a matter of vital importance to the State; the province of life or death; the road to survival or ruin. It is mandatory that it be thoroughly studied." My commentary follows his statements by showing applications for running a digital-age business. The same pattern is used in the rest of the chapters.

† Source: American Productivity & Quality Center and Product Development Institute.

- Defensive campaigns to hold an existing market position and make it more defensible.
- Campaigns to expand into new markets against entrenched competitors.

Sun Tzu describes what must be thoroughly studied.

> *Evaluate five fundamental factors and make comparisons: morale, weather, terrain, command, and doctrine.*
> *By morale I mean that which causes the staff to be in harmony with its leaders, so that they will accompany them without fear or feelings of insecurity.*

One of the primary approaches to keep "staff … in harmony with its leaders" is through empowerment. This is especially so with management's current emphasis on inclusion, participation, and collaboration. It is one of the most valuable and productive leadership strategies for the digital age.

The essential point: Within a technology-driven and volatile marketplace, relying on oneself to make rational decisions can be overwhelming and often counter-productive, whereas actively embracing empowerment as a primary requirement of leadership improves your chances of making accurate decisions.

When people are empowered with freedom of speech and thought, their minds tend to be flexible and inventive. "We are not very organized. It's intentional, it allows us to always keep our mind open to new ideas, ready to jump on new trends and take new opportunities," declared L'Oréal CEO Jean-Paul Agon.*

Otherwise, in a structured, top-down, command-and-control environment, freedom of expression is often stifled, and people's minds become rigid, regimented, and unresponsive.

> *By weather I mean the interaction of natural forces; the effects of winter's cold and summer's heat and the conduct of campaigns according to the seasons.*

---

* Excerpt from *Managing L'Oréal's Organized Chaos*, Fortune March 15, 2017 issue, p. 26–27.

This estimate focuses on the consequences of natural climate-related conditions. It influences how you manage your business within the variables of weather and logistics, such as seasonal outcomes of winter's cold and summer's heat.

IBM aids companies "according to the seasons" by providing retailers with weather data to guide business decisions for adjusting store merchandise based on forecasts over specific 48-hour periods.

Caterpillar utilizes predictive diagnostic tools to organize the enormous quantities of data spewing from sensors implanted in its equipment. In the "conduct of campaigns," the data helps its customers detect maintenance issues. Result: downtime is minimized, efficiency improves, productivity increases, and profitability soars.

> *By terrain I mean distances, whether the ground is crossed with ease or difficulty, if it is open or blocked, and the chances of success or failure.*

Within today's markets, "distances" are characterized by the increasing use of drones and the impending impact of autonomous vehicles. And distances are more realistically defined by cultural gaps and changes in buyer behavior that need to be "crossed with ease or difficulty."

Terrain also requires that you and your staff look with an entrepreneurial-focused, wide-vision lens at markets and determine whether they are "open or blocked" for entry. These, then, become the focal point for identifying new opportunities and developing winning strategies.

> *By command I mean the leader's qualities of wisdom, sincerity, humanity, courage, and strictness.*

Another dimension can be added to "the leader's qualities," which is gaining increasing attention: *influencing* staff by providing them with *purpose*.

"Purpose motivates employees better than profit," declared Feike Sijbesma.* Purpose can unite your staff in a common outlook. And when

---

* Feike Sijbesma, CEO of DSM, a Dutch nutrition and materials company, in 2014 made a breakthrough by cracking the bioengineering code to convert fibrous, woody biomass to fuel.

that collaborative effect occurs, the inhibiting result of organizational silos breaks down.

The outcome: a dynamic interplay of fresh business initiatives emerges that leads to new products and additional revenue streams.

Purpose varies, from IBM helping high schools with minimal resources close the technological skills gap and JPMorgan reviving a bankrupt industrial city, to Levi Strauss making a better life for the garment workers who make its jeans in other countries.

Such attachments are not all charitable. Often, they produce tangible bottom-line results to the organization, such as embedding a brand name within a new customer segment or achieving a publicity triumph in social media.

> *By doctrine I mean organization, control, appropriate assignments to managers, regulation of supply routes, and providing needed resources for the organization.*

Doctrine links with policy. Sun Tzu's definition is all encompassing and covers the foundation guidelines that control your organization or business unit. It forms a tangible imprint of your company's ethical and operating procedures.

Policy gives your organization consistency and a distinctive personality. It therefore has a legitimate and powerful grasp of your business plans and your ability to cultivate the natural growth of the market.

Alphabet (the parent company of Google) expresses its personality in its corporate manual, which states that the company would not focus on short-term profitability and would invest in employee rewards.

The document further explains the company's forward-thinking vision and corporate culture by declaring that it would invest in businesses well beyond internet search, even in areas that may seem speculative or strange.

The company did so by reaching far outside its core business to include YouTube and Android, as well as moves into artificial intelligence, hardware, entertainment, telecommunications, and media. These forays, some successful, others not, displayed a level of audacity and boldness as Alphabet explored such challenging areas as Google Glass, autonomous cars, energy-generating kites, all-terrain robots, delivery drones, seawater-based fuels, and smart contact lenses.

> *There is no leader who has not heard of these five matters. Those who master them win; those who do not are defeated.*

One of the potentially fatal outcomes of failing to pay attention to these "five matters" is being *too late*: too late in responding to aggressive competitors; too late in preparing growth strategies; too late in obtaining input from the staff that could reverse a downward slide; too late in reacting to evolving technology trends. Just being too late.

Outcome: you risk subsisting with a business model of playing catch-up, or worse, languishing with limited growth potential.

2

Developing Plans

Sun Tzu

Therefore, in developing plans compare the following elements, appraising them with the utmost care:

If you say which leader possesses moral influence and is more able, which organization obtains the advantages of nature and the terrain,

which group is better at carrying out instructions,

which individuals are the stronger,

which has the better trained managers and staff,

which administers rewards and punishments in a more rational manner,

I will be able to forecast which side will succeed and which will fail.

APPLICATIONS

Two of the above factors warrant commentary: training and rewards.

Training. Where empowerment is embedded in the organization, you should expect those individuals to think like strategists. For that reason, elevate the level of training so that they can fully apply their unique skills and talents to activate the corporate vision with an entrepreneurial focus.

Therefore, emphasize such internal and external topics as

- Changing demographics
- Shifting buying patterns
- Data analytics and artificial intelligence
- Globalization of markets and trade issues
- Saturated markets and new market development
- Aggressive competitors
- Rapid technological change
- Short product life cycles and new product development
- Mobile communications/social media
- Corporate culture and its effect on strategy

The essential point: Simply declaring to your staff that they are empowered is not likely to prove productive. You may receive scattered ideas of questionable relevance to the problems you currently face.

Thus, the "better trained" staff can more readily embrace the corporate vision, internalize the importance of influence and shared responsibility, practice strategy excellence, and mentally assume a mindset that relates to organizational agility.

Rewards. Of all the rewards, it is the longing for honor, recognition, and reputation that inspires individuals. There may be other compelling emotions, but rarely is there a substitute for renown, which is driven by an individual's innate ambition.

Psychologists have shown that people often value status over monetary rewards. The object of these cravings is to satisfy the deep-seated human need for prominence, recognition, self-esteem, reputation, and fame.

Psychologists further point out that individuals possess a strong inherent desire to distinguish themselves, driven by an intense urge to excel over others. Thus, the quest for social distinction is taken as a hardwired trait of human nature, which is satisfied by plaques, decorations, prizes, titles, and other tributes.

> *If a leader who listens to my strategy is employed, he is certain to win. Retain him! When one refuses to listen to my strategy is employed, he is certain to be defeated. Dismiss him!*

A qualifier is needed for Sun Tzu's abrupt comment to "dismiss him." It is in your best interests to determine why that individual "refuses to listen." Could it be imprecise communications, your leadership, a flaw in the strategy that needs to be explained, or other circumstances?

The premise is that all individuals have intrinsic value, such as unique skills and talents formed through cultural background, formal education, and life's experiences. Consequently, every effort should be made to harness their creative thinking and inventiveness to activate change and secure competitive advantage.

The central idea is to make empowerment work for you. That means, if you expect meaningful input from your people, it will come about only if you create a work environment wherein members of your staff can openly express their individuality.

> *Having paid attention to the advantages of my plans, the leader must create situations which will contribute to their accomplishment. By situations I mean that he should act expediently according to what is advantageous, and thereby control the balance.*

"Situations ... according to what is advantageous" are best achieved when you involve your staff to a point where they live in tune with their surroundings. Specifically, get them to an expanded state of *awareness* of the wider competitive world. Use internal communications, informal meetings, and weekly or monthly briefings to update your staff about markets, industries, and competitive conditions.

These get-togethers will be worth your time and effort as they serve several purposes:

- Tap into their diversity, experiences, and collective knowledge, thereby integrating individuals and their functions
- Obtain their viewpoints, which can provide useful perspectives and constructive comparisons
- Bring unity to your group
- Provide your staff with substantive market data and competitor information to think strategically

Such sessions help "control the balance" by awakening staff to the numerous visible and unforeseen obstacles. As one bank executive points out, "We spend a lot of time listening to team members through town-hall meetings, roundtables, and surveys. And we are very good at following up on the feedback we receive."

Doing so also allows you to focus individuals' attention on constructive projects, such as taking even a sketchy idea that may have been hatched through big data and converting it into a new product or service. Consequently, there is the exciting possibility that an embryonic innovation will sprout into a new revenue stream.

> *All confrontations are based on deception.*

Sun Tzu focuses on the nature of conflict, which he says has its roots in "deception."

On the surface, his compelling statement would appear to sound like a game of trickery layered with underhanded and secret maneuvering. If examined more deeply, Sun Tzu's meaning of deception forms the underpinnings for today's usage of disruptions, innovations, and initiatives that result in competitive advantage.

It shows itself when issuing false signals to competitors about your plans, or launching a product to pre-empt a rival's entry, or springing a sudden promotional campaign to unbalance the competitor and create surprise.

Therefore, think of deception not with any negative meaning. Instead, accept the more reliable interpretation as the application of Sun Tzu's concept of indirect strategy, which will be covered more fully further on.

The following statements describe Sun Tzu's application of deception.

> *When capable, pretend incapacity; when active, inactive.*
> *When near, make it appear that you are far away; when far away, that you are near.*
> *Offer the rival bait to lure him; simulate disorder and blunt his efforts.*
> *When he concentrates, prepare against him; where he is strong, avoid him.*
> *Anger his leader and confuse him.*
> *Pretend weakness and encourage his overconfidence.*
> *Keep him under a strain and wear him down.*
> *When he is united, divide him.*

> *Move when he is unprepared; venture forth when he does not expect you.*
> *These are the strategist's keys to victory. It is not possible to discuss them beforehand.*

Sun Tzu summarizes the chapter with the following statement:

> *Now if the estimates made before implementing a plan indicate victory, it is because calculations show one's strength to be superior to that of his rival. If they indicate defeat, it is because calculations show that one is inferior.*
>
> *With many calculations, one can win; with few one cannot. How much less chance of victory has one who makes none! By this means I examine the situation and the outcome will be clearly apparent.*

3

Victory

Sun Tzu

Victory is the main object of campaigns. If long delayed, budgets are consumed, morale depressed, and the staff's strength will be exhausted. When the company engages in long drawn-out campaigns the resources of the organization will not suffice.

APPLICATIONS

There are several issues in Sun Tzu's comment that should impact your thinking:

First, he points out that "victory is the main object of campaigns." This comment parallels what the late business scholar Peter Drucker astutely stated: "the object of business is to create a customer." Victory, in turn, is also determined by such metrics as return-on-investment, market share, profits, revenues, and the like.

Second, there is another dimension to victory. If it is long-delayed and becomes a prolonged effort, such as drawn-out marketing campaigns that consume operating budgets and demoralize employees, then severe problems result that can diminish any positive outcome. The draining of physical and financial resources that cannot be readily replaced can, in extreme cases, result in the demise of an organization.

The solution: From virtually every field of endeavor, speed surfaces as the single most important element for successfully implementing a strategy. This remedy does not mean reckless or impulsive movement. It does forewarn, however, that once careful and prudent estimates have been made, hesitation and indecision become your enemies.

For instance, speed impacts several managerial, organizational, and competitive issues, including

- How you communicate within your organization, so that decisions do not get stuck, distorted, or misinterpreted through layers of managers
- How fast you react to an aggressive competitor, where the clear-cut aim is to feed-off your customers, latch on to your supply chain, or erode your market position
- How rapidly you set your plan in motion, so that you are not reacting with hasty, impulsive movements
- How quickly you can launch a new product to gain a competitive edge and secure a favorable share-of-mind position among early adopters
- How rapidly you harness the digital technologies and integrate them into your internal operations, so that there is a favorable impact on customer solutions
- How fast you adopt new systems to foster virtual communications within your organization and along the entire supply chain

In contrast, delays, whether they are organizational patterns of behavior or sudden and unexpected events, affect many internal functions of the organization and influence your ability to manage employees effectively. Externally, sluggishness and a lack of urgency to react leaves an opening for an alert competitor to exploit.

Therefore, learning to act with rapid action and quick response to an opportunity or threat improves your market position, as opposed to slow, deliberate, and potentially ruinous hesitations.

Speed, then, offers the indispensable advantage of conserving precious resources from being dissipated over prolonged and arduous campaigns. Also, you gain the personal advantage of sustaining your employees' morale with decisive action.

Sun Tzu emphatically restates his comments about the dangers of long delays.

When your defenses are dulled, and enthusiasm damped, your strength exhausted, and resources spent, rivals will take advantage of your distress to act. And even though you have astute advisors, none will be able to lay good plans for the future.

Thus, while we have heard of rapid success, we have not yet seen a clever operation that was prolonged. For there has never been a protracted campaign from which an organization has benefited.

"Rivals will take advantage of your distress to act" means that whatever your difficulties, aggressive competitors are looking for openings and are only too anxious to exploit your problems. Often, they rely on excellent market intelligence for signs of weakness before they act.

Telltale signs of distress show up as employees' complaints at meetings and trade shows, layoffs, closed offices, reduced advertising, protests from customers about service and delivery, and other explicit signals.

Thus, the draining of resources has irreparably damaged more companies than almost any other factor. And in tough economic times, it becomes increasingly difficult to replace people, where hiring freezes are in force and financing runs out.

For your purposes, therefore, extended deliberation without action, overall procrastination, and long chains of command from home office to the field are all detriments to success.

Sun Tzu extends his discussion of "a protracted campaign" with the following statement:

When an organization is impoverished by aggressive operations, it is due to maintaining activities over long distances.

The implication, here, is that a campaign that extends over distances has its own built-in momentum, which also diminishes in time and distance.

Thus, you have to know when to cease the offensive effort before the organization becomes "impoverished by aggressive operations" as resources and budgets are depleted. The object, then, is to avoid getting your firm or group into a state of exhaustion.

There are some campaigns that have led directly to the stated objective of the plan in an on-time, lock-step approach. But these are in the minority. Most campaigns only lead to the point where the available resources and budgets are just enough to stay marginally involved.

Beyond that point, the scale turns and the expenditures in time and effort don't produce a significant effect. In fact, continued attempts often become counter-productive. This is the essential meaning of the end point of the campaign. This is especially so when shaping strategies and committing any of your organization's resources against entrenched competitors.

Therefore, your task is to determine what represents the end point in a campaign. Would gaining an extra point of market share be worth the expenditures? Or would continuing the efforts and expending more resources place the entire campaign in doubt and result in exhausting financial, material, and personnel resources?

There are numerous factors that contribute to a decision to halt "aggressive operations." What matters, therefore, is to detect that point with discriminative judgment.

You can determine the end point by using quantitative calculations related to the plan's objectives, and by compiling a list of non-quantitative criteria, such as assessing the morale of staff and the likely reactions of competitors to continuing the campaign.

The following factors should help determine the end point:

1. You challenged the rival's strong areas but overspent unrecoverable resources. And it is possible the competitor has unused resources or receives additional budgetary commitments and can outspend you.

2. The moment you entered the competitor's market, operations changed. It became contested through claims and counter-claims, price wars, increasing promotional expenditures, and opposition that were totally unexpected.

3. You moved away from your primary supply chain, while the competitor tightened his relationships. This caused barriers to establishing new relationships.

4. There is danger of the rival receiving aid from venture capitalists, offers for joint ventures, and opportunities for mergers.

5. The competitor, facing heightened danger, makes a spirited effort to fight back, whereas your efforts slacken.

Finally, an answer may come to you intuitively through an inner voice that says, "It's time to end the campaign."

> *Hence, what is essential in all efforts is victory, not prolonged operations. And, therefore, the leader who understands conflict is the minister of the people's fate and authority of the organization's destiny.*

4

Employing Staff

Sun Tzu

Those unable to understand the dangers inherent in employing staff are equally unable to understand the advantageous ways of doing so.

APPLICATIONS

"Companies face more competition today than ever," according to Clifton Leaf, editor-in-chief of *Fortune*.* Yet some managers fail to "understand the dangers inherent in employing staff" when entering a highly competitive marketplace.

For the most part, it means using maneuver to overwhelm the competitor's resistance, and doing so without direct confrontation.

The essential technique is to deploy employees for maximum efficiency, which takes a good deal of preparation.

First, you need an all-inclusive framework consisting of the following areas:

- *Customers.* Infuse your staff with the rock-solid, irrefutable belief that customers know more about what they need than your people do. That means training them to lean heavily on core customers to assist in coming up with viable strategies.

---

* *Fortune*, August 1, 2018 issue, p. 6.

- *Networks.* Today's sophisticated information technology allows secure and fast links among customers, suppliers, business partners, and employees. Therefore, have your staff maintain a multi-directional flow of information with other groups, from initial product concept to its final delivery.
- *Alliances.* In the current scheme of organizational and business strategy, alliances and other forms of partnering serve as the foundations for success. To make the connections work, alert staff to the advantages of maintaining a seamless exchange of information by cultivating a high level of trust among various managerial levels to achieve agreed-upon short and long-term goals.
- *Corporate culture.* Your company's culture—formed by values, objects, history, ideas, and behavioral patterns—is expressed through supportive relationships, which not only reflect on customers and suppliers, but also show that your employees are intellectual assets to be nurtured and developed. Thus, indispensable to your organization is the ability to help them acquire a mindset that is totally customer driven.
- *Technology.* Digital technologies and the incoming applications of artificial intelligence are now integral components for shaping business strategies. Technology impacts directly on such basic functions as research and development (R&D), manufacturing, marketing, distribution, and customer service. It is in your best interests to form cross-functional teams and empower them. (See Table 4.1, Duties and Responsibilities of a Cross-Functional Team.)

Second, as for your leadership role to "understand the advantageous ways" of employing your staff, consider how you can shape your style by incorporating the following attributes: *astuteness*, *straightforwardness*, *compassion*, *boldness*, and *strictness*.

If *astute*, you anticipate early on the eventual impact of new competitive intrusions, customers' changing behaviors, industry disruptions, and technological issues. Once noted, you can act rapidly and boldly to create opportunities and diffuse threats.

If *straightforward*, personnel have no doubt about how and when you hand out rewards—or reprimands.

If *compassionate*, you show respect for people, appreciate their commitment and hard work, and empathize with them in difficult situations.

TABLE 4.1

Duties and Responsibilities of a Cross-Functional Team

General functions include:

- Aligning the organization's or business unit's broad vision with the new possibilities resulting from digitization
- Utilizing big data when assessing the environmental, technological, industry, customer, and competitor situations
- Developing long and short-term objectives and strategies based on predictive analytics
- Preparing product, market, supply chain, and quality plans to implement competitive strategies
- Maintaining a viable competitive market position by means of offensive and defensive strategies

Responsibilities include:

- Recommending new or modified products and services
- Planning strategies throughout the product life cycle that utilize big data and analytics to determine courses of action that can be implemented with speed at decisive points
- Developing tactical plans to secure markets against competitive threats
- Identifying product and service opportunities in light of changing consumer buying patterns resulting from the outputs of data analytics
- Collaborating with various corporate functions to achieve short and long-term objectives
- Organizing inter-divisional exchanges of new market or product opportunities through the internal company communications network
- Cooperating in developing a strategic business plan for a business unit or product line so that it aligns with the corporate culture

If *bold*, you gain market advantage by seizing opportunities without hesitation.

If *strict*, you are dedicated to the vision and objectives of the organization. In turn, personnel are respectful of all these strong-minded attributes.

Sun Tzu then focuses on one quality, customers, which incorporates many of the above attributes:

> *Treat customers well, and care for them. This is called winning a battle and becoming stronger.*

John Deere, the farm equipment manufacturer, illustrates how to "treat customers well" and "understand the advantageous ways" of employing staff. Executives put together teams of assembly-line workers and had them crisscross North America and talk to dealers and farmers about

Deere's farm equipment. Many of the workers involved in the effort had over 15 years with the company.

They traveled in small groups and pitched their product stories to farmers at regional trade exhibits. Some workers from specialized job functions routinely made unscheduled visits to local farmers to discuss their problems and needs. In most places, they were accepted as friendly, non-threatening individuals who had no ulterior motives other than to present an honest, grass-roots account of what goes into making a quality Deere product.

Underlying the workforce strategy was Deere's customer-first approach and the advantages of employing staff: All employees are considered valuable resources to serve the needs of customers. As such, they were trained in advanced manufacturing methods, total quality programs, and teamwork. According to Deere's management, harnessing that expertise demonstrated to customers that, as makers of the products, they were the best company spokespeople.

From Deere's viewpoint, a great deal was accomplished: customers' problems were identified early on, as well as likely threats from competitors. The physical acts of working closely with customers uncovered potential new benefits that could be considered back at the home office.

Consequently, empowering the company's workforce achieved a major benefit by supporting its customer-loyalty efforts, which complemented Deere's core competencies, products, services, and cultural values. All this information was internally communicated to deliver a powerful message of management–labor harmony, which kept in check possible areas of internal friction.

Altogether, the approach strengthened customer relationships by capitalizing on Deere's employees' experience, insight, and maturity. In turn, it resulted in another measurable outcome: a sharp increase in net income, along with sizable jumps in sales and market share over the following reporting period.

5

Offensive Strategy

Sun Tzu

Generally, in a competitive environment, the best policy is to take a market undamaged; to ruin it would be counter-productive.

APPLICATIONS

Translating Sun Tzu's "to take a market undamaged" means a profitable, environmentally cared for, and economically strong market over the long term. It represents a thriving arena anchored to stable customer relationships, with sensitivity to the grass-roots culture of each segment.

Conversely, combative sales tactics, predatory pricing, and waging continuous marketing warfare for every point of market share "would be counter-productive." Thus, any damage due to faulty products, inferior services, and aggressive sales tactics are shortsighted actions, particularly with today's focus on customer relationships as the centerpiece of business practice.

To subdue the competitor is better than to bankrupt it.

While you may wish to see your rival exit the market or simply go out of business, your primary interest should be in maintaining stability in the market and planning for its future growth. Therefore, think about encouraging the competing company to remain in the market, possibly confined to a segment that is in no direct threat to you, as the prudent choice.

> *For to win one hundred victories in one hundred encounters is not the peak of skill. To subdue the competitor without fighting is the peak of skill.*

That fighting "is not the peak of skill" is one of Sun Tzu's most enduring concepts. The clear inference is that clashes are destructive, consume valuable resources, and usually damage the bottom line of profitability.

Yet, if challenged in open and contentious market warfare, it is normal, and necessary, to respond by opposing or neutralizing aggressive tactics. Sun Tzu elaborates on how to deal with such issues in the following statements.

> *Thus, what is of supreme importance is to block the competitor's strategy.*

The object here is to unbalance the competing manager into making impulsive moves, which often results in costly mistakes. By interfering with a competitor's strategy, you throw the opposing manager into disarray and with it his ability to perform rationally.

Such wavering often results in hasty choices, such as ordering a premature launch of a new product, undertaking promotions without adequate analysis, or initiating a hasty redeployment of the sales force; the competing manager's ability to supply outlets could also be impaired. Therefore, attempting to create an unbalancing effect in a rival manager's thinking could cause fear and other negative emotions that result in damaging outcomes.

Consequently, when the competing manager feels trapped and unable to counter your moves quickly enough, he or she may make mistakes in judgment and thereby play into your hands.

Achieving surprise, then, is an integral component in your thinking about how to "block the competitor's strategy." It depends on a reliable estimate of what conditions would affect the competing manager's will to resist your actions.

Next best is to disrupt his alliances.

The ongoing trend of alliances, joint ventures, acquisitions, and the variety of creative partnering arrangements dominating today's business scene make this point particularly troublesome. Yet, even where competitors join against you, it is still possible to find soft spots in market coverage or weaknesses in their strategy.

To sit passively, however, could end up as an insurmountable problem because the sum of two competitors mounted against you would fortify their respective positions beyond your ability to defend.

Should an alliance develop, there is still time to exploit the newly formed coalition, especially if the respective managements experience difficulties finding a comfortable middle ground from which to operate in a unified manner. Then, there is the case where a company makes ill-advised acquisitions, as in the instance of General Electric; according to industry experts, this is what caused its decline.

Within those voids, it is possible to create opportunities by moving rapidly and devising upsetting obstacles. Such time intervals could prove invaluable for priming your creative thinking and devising new strategies.

The next best is to attack the competitor.

Attacking a competitor means neutralizing his or her strategy. Two broad areas are worth examining, providing you can outperform your rival: (1) increase customers' revenues; (2) decrease customers' costs.

To increase customers' revenue:

- Reduce customers' returns and complaints.
- Improve customers' market position and image.
- Create a brand strategy to improve customers' revenues.
- Collaborate with customers to uncover product or service benefits to bolster their competitiveness.
- Integrate technology advances to create possibilities for differentiation.
- Upgrade reordering procedures and speed up delivery to create a positive impact on revenues.

To decrease customers' costs:

- Decrease customers' purchase costs.
- Cut customers' production downtime.
- Reduce customers' delivery costs.
- Shrink customers' administrative overhead.
- Maximize customers' working capital.

Cargill, the largest privately held company in the United States, illustrates its version of how to "attack the competitor." For over 150 years, the Minnesota-based company provided its core customers—farmers—with data about commodity prices, storage facilities, and other middleman functions for the buying and selling of crops. Now, armed with a smartphone or a tablet, even the small farmer can get real-time data about weather conditions, market prices, and other vital information.

These disruptive changes have pushed Cargill to redefine itself from a trading company to an integrated food company as a supplier of ground beef and seafood. Yet, it remained close to its roots by embracing cutting-edge technologies to increase customers' revenue and decrease their costs.

Using sophisticated satellite photographs, it helps analyze crop conditions for farmers with a level of detail that was unimaginable a few years ago. The result: more precise predictions of the condition of crops near each of its grain elevators, which permits customized pricing and the possibility of maximizing profits.

Other initiatives include software that helps farmers identify individual cows by means of facial recognition gear that keeps track of what they eat. It also measures how much milk they produce to better manage a herd's productivity. "We are trying to bring digital transformation to the industry," says a Cargill executive.

> *The worst policy is to show aggressive tactics in a market. Attack only when there is no alternative.*

Sun Tzu continues his warning about the futility of open market warfare.

The better way: With the help of a team, study the market for weak spots that represent opportunities. These could be a market segment that is poorly served, a technology that focuses on a group of early adopters, or a product application that solves a current business problem.

Instagram, the photo-sharing app, had to resolve a competitive problem during one of its challenging periods: how to uncover a way to introduce e-commerce features without copying the common approach of using pop-up ads. To find answers, individuals from the management and technical ranks found a solution: let brands tag their products to the photos they post, like the way users tag their friends.

The team also discussed other features for future add-ons, such as a product-search feature, a way to comparison shop, and a means to provide posts that could feature various objects. Looking to the future, the team also considered Instagram's overall corporate vision and how the company was positioned in the marketplace. The group did not want to be caught napping and have "to attack a market."

If the leader is unable to control his impatience and orders his staff to prematurely implement a plan, much resources will be lost without achieving the objectives. Such is the calamity of these campaigns.

While speed and correct timing are critical to success, impatience and lack of preparation are detriments to a profitable outcome. Sun Tzu's point has far-reaching effects, as illustrated by Microsoft's CEO Satya Nadella.

A research project caught Nadella's attention: A demonstration that used speech recognition and artificial intelligence to translate a live conversation into another language. Immediately noticing the commercial possibilities, Nadella wanted the tool combined with Skype as a working prototype.

Ordinarily, the task takes a great deal of slow and methodical preparation — often a year or more. Working at crisis-level speed, the responsible business unit immediately assembled a team and went to work to meet the deadline. The resulting product: the Skype Translator, which eventually became available in numerous languages.

The essential point: To prevent "calamity of these campaigns," three conditions are needed: a lean and responsive organization, a customer-centric culture, and an empowered staff. Each of these prerequisites existed at Microsoft, where organizational agility and empowerment are embedded in the corporation's operating culture. Thus, any semblance of impatience was a non-issue.

6

Skill in Strategy

Sun Tzu

Those skilled in strategy subdue the competitor without direct confrontation. They capture its markets without drawn-out operations.

APPLICATIONS

What does "skilled in strategy" mean in today's competitive world?

In its broadest sense, strategy encompasses numerous internal and external issues, which must be considered to reduce the risk of getting entangled in "drawn-out operations."

These issues encompass all aspects of digital technologies, especially the enormous impact that artificial intelligence, the Internet of Things, robotics, machine learning, and data analytics will have on your business.

Best Buy, the electronics retailer, was concerned with a few of the above issues. Its managers looked at an emerging and highly attractive demographic market for geriatric-care products.

Market analytics confirmed that by 2020, about 45 million Americans will be caring for 117 million seniors, spending on everything from food delivery to safety and health monitors. Adding to the market's attractiveness were survey data that showed 90% of seniors wanted to stay at home.

Why, then, with such a bright market outlook, should Best Buy leaders be anxious? Facing the company were aggressive giants, such as Google, Microsoft, and Samsung. All their executives were reading the same glowing statistics. They, too, savored a leading position in the smart-home market with networked gear, such as security cameras and thermostats that can be managed by voice controllers or smartphones.

For Best Buy, following Sun Tzu's advice to "subdue the competitor without direct confrontation" would have meant training personnel to selectively incorporate the above areas of strategy into their responses to each competitor.

> *Your aim must be to achieve your market objectives unharmed. That is, your staff is not worn out, and your gains are complete. This is the art of offensive strategy.*

Making certain that your company remains "unharmed" after conducting an offensive strategy means that your staff is "not worn out" physically. One reason for singling out physical effort is that it is one of the great sources of internal friction. The problem, however, is that the limits of physical energy by personnel under prolonged and stressful conditions are exceedingly hard to gauge.

Yet, if left unattended, the consequences of fatigue are certain to impact employees' morale and their abilities to make coherent decisions. It is also unlikely that you can "achieve your market objectives."

As Sun Tzu points out in a later section: "Pay heed to nourishing the staff; do not unnecessarily fatigue them. Unite them in spirit; conserve their strength."

Organizations respond in various ways to the issue of how their staffs relate to expending physical energy. Their approaches consider attitudes, morale, and physical and mental well-being. They also include creature comforts, pathways to professional growth, and confident feelings about job security.

Thus, protecting them, nurturing them, and enhancing their intrinsic capabilities so they develop into top-performing and skilled individuals legitimately ranks among a leader's top priorities.

Sun Tzu goes on to describe a variety of conditions which deal with the use of personnel.

Consequently, the art of using your staff is this:
When ten to the competitor's one, surround him.
When five times his strength, attack him.
If double his strength, divide him.
If equally matched, engage him.
If weaker numerically, withdraw from him.
And if in all respects unequal, elude him; for a small force is but
booty for one more powerful.

The above statements are made from a perspective of protecting the organization, which is an awesome responsibility. At stake is the long-term viability of your firm, which begins and ends with those who consume your company's products or services: the customer.

The leader is the protector of the organization. If this protection is all-encompassing, the organization will be strong; if faulty, it will be weak.

Protection in its most practical sense means taking responsibility for nurturing the long-term growth of your market, retaining long-term customer relationships, and contributing to your organization's well-being. It also means taking responsibility for the prudent expenditures of financial, human, and material resources.

Conversely, protection is not achieved by costly encounters in the marketplace that often deteriorate into price wars and other confrontational tactics — unless all other options have been considered.

These points are summarized in the following principles:

- To succeed over a competitor through strength-conserving strategies is far better than forcing it out of business through combative marketing tactics.
- What is of supreme importance is to attack your competitor's strategy.
- If you resolve internal difficulties before they arise, you win. If you decrease a competitor's threat before it materializes, you win. And if you overcome customers' resistance and solve their problems, you win.

- If you tune in to customers' needs and behaviors through all the touch points of data, you then work at an advantage, providing you can translate the findings into new market and product opportunities.
- If you succeed in disrupting a competitor's alliance, you thereby reduce the potential impact of having to face a more formidable competitor.
- If you use employee empowerment as a force multiplier, the combined energies of those individuals are best suited to take advantage of technology breakthroughs to outthink, outmaneuver, and outperform competitors.

Sun Tzu continues:

> *There are four ways in which a leader can bring misfortune upon his organization or business group:*
> *When ignorant that the organization should not advance, the leader orders an advance; or ignorant that it should not retreat, orders a retreat. This means unbalancing the organization.*
> *When the leader is ignorant of business affairs, to participate in their administration. This confuses personnel.*

General Electric CEO John Flannery, who succeed outgoing Jeff Immelt in 2017, provides a comprehensive definition of what is understood as "business affairs":

"We evaluate our businesses, processes, (the) corporate (function), our culture, how decisions are made, how we think about goals and accountability, how we incentivize people, how we prioritize investments in the segments … global research, digital, and manufacturing. We review our operating processes, our team, capital allocation, and how we communicate to investors. Everything is on the table."

> *When ignorant of command problems, to share in its responsibilities. This engenders doubts in the minds of the staff.*

If the staff is confused and suspicious, competitors will cause trouble. This is what is meant by, a confused staff leads to another's victory.

Leadership is all about responsibility, accountability, and achieving objectives. Leaders inspire their people, organize actions, and respond to market and competitive uncertainty with speed and effectiveness. Therefore, any manager "ignorant of command problems" or anyone who causes his staff to be "confused and suspicious" can bring "misfortune upon his organization."

Taking it a step further, it is no giant leap for personnel to think their leader is ineffective and unable to motivate people to action. Therefore, make every effort to keep employees tuned in to evolving events.

Listen to their comments and gain a sense of their conversations. Then verify information that is true, uncover false information, and immediately squelch unfounded rumors with qualified information.

There are five circumstances in which triumph may be predicted. It is in these five matters that the way to victory is known:

> *He who knows when he can fight and when he cannot will be victorious.*
> *He who understands how to use both large and small forces will be victorious.*
> *He whose ranks are united in purpose will be victorious.*
> *He who is prudent and lies in wait for a competitor who is not, will be victorious.*
> *He whose leaders are able and not interfered with by those at the senior level will be victorious.*

The following statement is one of Sun Tzu's widely quoted statements. In a few words, he expresses the vital importance that market intelligence has in laying plans for offensive strategy. The advice takes on even more importance with the advances in this age of big data and artificial intelligence.

Therefore, I say: Know the competitor and know yourself; in a hundred battles you will never be in peril.

When you are ignorant of the competitor, but know yourself, your chances of winning or losing are equal.

If ignorant both of your competitor and of yourself, you are certain in every conflict to be in peril.

7

Dispositions

Sun Tzu

Individuals skilled in strategy make themselves invincible and await the rival's moment of vulnerability.

Invincibility depends on one's self; the rival's vulnerability on him.

It follows that those skilled in conflict can make themselves invincible, but cannot cause a rival to be totally vulnerable.

APPLICATIONS

Levi Strauss & Co., the creator of the famous Levi jeans, illustrates what happened during the period of finding itself vulnerable, and its attempt to become invincible. The company participated in the fashion explosion of the 21st century, when denim jeans became a basic item for tens of millions of individuals worldwide. It also exposed Levi's vulnerability.

With the continuing trend of vast numbers of individuals wearing jeans, the inevitable parade of competitors followed, as in the likes of Lee, Wrangler, and others trying to cash in on the continuing movement. What resulted was intense competition for Levi, with the outcome that sales nosedived for an extended period.

Then other factors surfaced that furthered the decline. Internally, Levi's design team was too late in latching on to key trends. More fundamental issues appeared, such as a lack of discipline and the inability to correctly identify decisive segments on which to concentrate resources.

What was as serious was that some senior-level executives, by their own admission, acted as if they had a monopoly on the denim market and took little notice when young fashion-conscious individuals began trading in their Levi's for more trendy styles offered by start-up rivals.

As one executive pointed out, "We have one of the greatest brands in the world, but I think that there may have been periods where we thought the brand itself could carry us through thick and thin. There's no question that we got complacent."

As Sun Tzu points out, "Invincibility depends on one's self." Thus, a recovery process began as key executives traveled to the company's world-wide offices and interviewed senior managers about what immediate changes could make a difference. Result: New teams were formed that addressed sensitive issues, such as improving internal communications, revitalizing morale, and casting off negative feelings that caused complacency.

Management then addressed the all-important matter of marketing the iconic Levi brand, which had been woefully neglected. That meant implementing a bold effort by launching a campaign highlighting the company's legacy as the inventor of blue jeans.

> *Invincibility lies in the defense; the possibility of victory in the attack.*
>
> *One defends when his strength is inadequate; he attacks when it is abundant.*

To apply Sun Tzu's points about defense and attack, consider the advantages and disadvantages of defending what already exists vs. going on the offensive to exploit new market opportunities.

ADVANTAGES OF DEFENSE

The object of defense is first, to preserve a market position against the inroads of competitors; second, to maintain positive relationships with customers; and third, to protect the organization's reputation, image, and brand, as well as any intellectual property that would represent a unique and sustainable advantage. Should any of these areas reach the point of being in jeopardy, then the viability of the organization, business unit, or product line could be vulnerable.

Thus, it is also more advantageous to hold a well-entrenched position than to take a new one. And it is far more profitable to retain existing customers than pay heavily to acquire new ones.

The essential point: Relying totally on defense is contrary to growth over the long term, so that, "One defends when his strength is inadequate," and "attack when it is abundant"—that is, as described in the Levi Strauss case, as soon as there is a strong enough capability to actively pursue a positive objective. One cannot attain any successful outcome from a campaign by staying totally on the defensive.

ADVANTAGES OF THE OFFENSIVE

Maneuver and diversion are the key advantages of the offensive. Both aim to bring about favorable conditions for success. First, the offensive forces the competitor to scatter its resources; second, it identifies where to concentrate your next efforts.

Further, offensive moves tend to surprise and unbalance the defender. They thereby afford excellent possibilities, especially where the defender has a cumbersome organization with layers of management that prevents quick decisions, and where the defender's morale is at a vulnerable point.

Consequently, the offensive becomes a constant interchange and combination of offense and defense. Accordingly, every offensive action will likely end in a defense decided by any of the conditions described above.

With the following statements, Sun Tzu continues with invincibility and vulnerability by citing the attributes of a leader.

> *To foresee a victory which the ordinary person can foresee is not the acme of skill.*
>
> *To triumph in a campaign and be a universally acclaimed 'Expert' is not the acme of skill.*

Those called skilled in confrontations, conquer a rival easily conquered.

He wins his victories without erring. Without erring means that whatever he does insures his victory; he conquers a rival already defeated.

Therefore, the skillful leader takes up a position in which he cannot be defeated and misses no opportunity to master his foe.

Thus, a victorious organization wins its victories before seeking conflict; a rival destined to defeat fights in the hope of winning.

Most of Sun Tzu's previous statements describe what needs to be studied, such as what comparisons are necessary, what situations must be created to achieve success, how to use deception as the key to victory, the value of speed, what intelligence is needed in laying plans, and the value of subduing the competitor without fighting as the peak of skill.

In the following statements, Sun Tzu graphically describes the effects of preparation before any conflict begins.

Now, the elements of the art of conflict are first, measurement of space; second, estimation of quantities; third, calculations; fourth, comparisons; and fifth, chances of victory.

Thus, a victorious force is as a hundredweight balanced against a grain; a defeated group as a grain balanced against a hundredweight.

It is because of disposition that a victorious leader can make his people fight with the effect of pent-up waters which, suddenly released, plunge into a bottomless chasm.

8

Energy

Sun Tzu

Generally, management of many is the same as management of few. It is a matter of organization.

And to control many is the same as to control few.

APPLICATIONS

Managing and controlling personnel through empowerment is the essence of successful leadership for the digital age. Empowerment was mentioned numerous times in previous chapters.

It is repeated once again to align with Sun Tzu's theme of "management of many is the same as management of few." The emphasis here is on tapping into the treasure trove of human intelligence and utilizing the wealth of experience lodged within your staff.

The key point: Empowerment is driven by *influence*, which depends on the personality of each member of your staff to function as a leader. That means the power of influence goes beyond a person's direct control, job title, or position on the organization chart.

Expressed another way: Influence is not defined by span of control; it doesn't have that restriction. The only important considerations are how extensive the influences are, how many individuals actively embrace the organization's strategic vision, and how meaningful their contributions are.

Then, there is another reality about empowerment: Not all individuals in a group can be reached and influenced through words, rewards, or financial incentives. Negativity may surface that is clearly counterproductive to your efforts.

What is needed is education and training to expose these individuals and others to the skills, mindsets, and attributes of leadership. That includes sharing goals in a language with which they can identify.

Your aim, then, is to maintain this pyramid effect that keeps the process growing, and where others willingly continue the effort. Making it all work is an organizational culture that permits empowerment to exist.

> *That the organization is certain to sustain the competitor's aggressive efforts without suffering defeat is due to operations of the extraordinary and the normal forces.*
>
> *Generally, use the normal force to engage; use the extraordinary to win.*

The normal and extraordinary are likened to the indirect strategy, which was initially introduced by Sun Tzu in Chapter 2 as *all confrontations are based on deception* with the intent of avoiding direct confrontation.

The indirect strategy operates along five dimensions:

First, the strategy consists of a series of actions whereby you apply your strengths against a competitor's weaknesses. The essence of the move is that you cleverly position your resources so that your rival cannot, or will not, challenge your efforts.

Second, concurrent with activating indirect moves against a competitor, your focus should be directed toward serving customers' needs and resolving their problems in an extraordinary manner that outperforms those of your competitors.

Third, your aim is to achieve a psychological advantage by creating an unbalancing effect in the rival manager's mind, whereby he or she vacillates in indecision. The effect is to disorient and unbalance the competing manager into wasting time and making costly and irreversible mistakes.

Fourth, your purpose is to convince your competitor that continuing aggressive efforts will be too costly, with little chance of justifying the expenditures of people, money, and materials.

Fifth, fighting in the marketplace is not your intention. Rather, your aim is *possession*. That is, your purpose is to hold a long-term position in a growing market.

Sun Tzu imaginatively describes the boundless opportunities to develop extraordinary forces.

The resources of those skilled in the use of extraordinary forces are as infinite as the heavens and earth; as inexhaustible as the flow of the great rivers.

The musical notes are only five in number, but their melodies are so numerous that one cannot hear them all.
The primary colors are only five in number, but their combinations are so infinite that one cannot visualize them all.
The flavors are only five in number, but their blends are so various that one cannot taste them all.

In confrontations, there are only the normal and extraordinary forces, but their combinations are limitless; none can comprehend them all.

These two forces are mutually reproductive; their interactions are as endless as that of interlocked rings. Who can determine where one ends and the other begins?

With so much at stake when entering a market and confronting competition, your success depends on overriding the numerous obstacles by means of maneuver. Thus, a conscious awareness of the indirect strategy, and the normal and extraordinary forces, is the mindset you need to establish with empowered individuals.

The aim is to tap into their limitless imaginings and creative thinking. It is the one dominant approach that determines if your organization grows and prospers—or if it languishes as an also-ran. Thus, where maneuverability is needed and where it is skillfully applied, "the resources of those skilled in the use of extraordinary forces are as infinite as the heavens and earth."

Order or disorder depends on organization; courage or coward-ice on circumstances; strength or weakness on dispositions.

Thus, those skilled in making the rival move do so by creating a situation to which he must conform; they entice him with some-thing he is certain to take, and with lures of ostensible profit they await him in strength.

Therefore, a skilled leader seeks victory from the situation and does not demand it of his subordinates.
He selects his people and they exploit the situation.

All the above comments relate to leadership, especially where empowerment is in place. One of Sun Tzu's statements, however, can be singled out for commentary: "a skilled leader seeks victory from the situation and does not demand it of his subordinates."

The following represent likely situations for your staff to exploit:

- Situations to defend a market position

  Protecting a market position is the primary objective of defense. Here is where your team can develop counter-strategies to block the aggressive moves of a competitor.
- Situations to exploit a competitor's weakness

  These represent the most likely areas of a rival's vulnerability, such as poor product quality, inadequate back-up service, lapses in technology, problems with the supply chain, or inept leadership. Wherever you can draw out the creativity of individuals with exper-tise in any of those fields, your chances of winning improve.
- Situations created through joint-venture agreements

  It is becoming increasingly difficult to enter a market alone and expect to succeed. Of necessity, various types of joint relationships are needed to fill in gaps, such as adding more product lines, offer-ing support services, and inserting new levels of technology. Other joint relationships may be formed to reach specialized geographic markets, or to network into other industries and companies.
- Situations to expand into additional market niches against dominant competitors

The key point here is to locate a decisive point through which to enter a market against embedded rivals. It is the most effective point in which to concentrate your resources. Here, again, your staff would exploit the competitor's general area of vulnerability.

- Situations to make a confrontation costlier for the rival to continue operations

The issue here is how to influence your competitor's expenditures, so that prolonging a campaign would make the effort costlier in terms of human, material, and financial resources. Further, the ongoing drain of reserves is likely to create undue stress and cause rival executives to make irreversible mistakes.

9

Weaknesses and Strengths

Sun Tzu

Generally, he who occupies the market first and awaits his competitors is at ease; he who comes later to the scene and rushes into the fray is weary.

APPLICATIONS

While it is beneficial to be first in with an innovation and become a dominant player in a market segment, there are also disadvantages. The classic case of Xerox illustrates Sun Tzu's point.

Decades ago, when Xerox created the market for xerography, the company initially focused on large companies with its large copiers. If we introduce Sun Tzu's concept of "awaits his competitors ... at ease," it would appear that Xerox's management misinterpreted his comment and adopted a passive defense.

That is, Xerox relied primarily on a sterling reputation and its dominance among the world's largest organizations. Meanwhile, deliberately or accidently, it left exposed a vast market of small- and midsize companies for small, tabletop copiers. In effect, it had no active plan to cover possible segments of vulnerability.

Astute Japanese makers of copiers, such as Canon, Sharp, and Ricoh, saw the opening and attacked that vacant market with virtually no opposition. Securing a solid foothold in North America, they made the next expansive move by going against Xerox's stronghold in big companies. Had those companies initially entered the copier market at the large company segment, they would have come "into the fray ... weary."

Thus, defending one's territory is certainly a prudent strategy. However, it must be actively defended.

In the following statements, Sun Tzu explains the meaning of an active defense:

> *Those skilled in conflicts bring the rival to the market and are not brought there by him.*
>
> *One able to make the rival come of his own accord does so by offering him some advantage. And one able to prevent him from coming does so by hurting him.*
>
> *When the competitor is at ease, be able to weary him; when at rest, make him move.*
>
> *Appear at places to which he must hasten; move swiftly where he does not expect you.*
>
> *To be certain to take what you attack is to attack a place the rival does not protect. To be certain to hold what you defend is to defend a place the competitor does not strike.*
>
> *Therefore, against those skilled in attack, a competitor does not know where to defend; against the experts in defense, the rival does not know where to attack.*

If Xerox's management thought its dominant position was sustainable, that notion proved unrealistic, whereas it would have been totally realistic to expect rivals to enter a growth market. The issue, then, for Xerox to maintain control, would require its managers to shift from offensive to defensive strategies and vice versa as market conditions changed.

Again, using Sun Tzu's guidelines, a possible scenario would have had the Xerox management setting up a team to produce, or contract outside for, small copiers to block, or slow down, the rivals' efforts. Other groups would disrupt the distribution network of retail stores that served the small company market with office equipment and supplies.

At the same time, Xerox's main strength would focus on defending its position in the large copier market through ongoing product modifications and marketing efforts. Thus, being active means constant attention to strengths and weaknesses.

When I wish to avoid conflict, I may defend myself simply by drawing a line on the ground; the rival will be unable to attack because I divert him from going where he wishes.

If I can determine the rival's dispositions while at the same time, I conceal my own, then I can concentrate, and he must divide.

And If I concentrate while he divides, I can use my entire strength to attack a fraction of his. There, I will be numerically superior.

Then, if I can use many to strike few at the selected point, those I deal with will be in dire straits.

The rival must not know where I intend to give battle. For if he does not know where I intend to give battle he must prepare in a great many places. And when he prepares in a great many places, those I must fight in any one place will be few.

Thus, I say that victory can be created. For even if the competitors are numerous, I can prevent them from engaging.

Therefore, determine the rival's plans and you will know which strategy will be successful and which will not.

Agitate him and ascertain the pattern of his movement.

Determine his dispositions and so ascertain the area to be contested.

Probe him and learn where his strength is abundant and where deficient.

Still applying Sun Tzu's statements to the Xerox case, had its management initiated a post-market review of the situation, the following seven questions would have proved relevant:

1. Was the threat to our position wholly unexpected? Could it have been avoided if we had a more agile organization that permitted the rapid flow of intelligence from the field to the appropriate decision-making managers? In turn, could we have responded rapidly when the Japanese companies entered the small business market?

2. Could we have averted the crisis if we had a strategic business plan that included counter-strategies that could be implemented rapidly?

3. To what extent did senior executives and line managers internalize the seriousness of an impending conflict with the Japanese companies?

4. Were junior managers—including those from sales—trained in developing offensive and defensive strategies to protect our core market position?

5. Did we have cross-functional teams at various levels with responsibilities to develop business plans? Were they empowered to act?

6. Did any of our senior executives and line managers show exceptional leadership to motivate individuals as well as deal with strength-draining emotions of fear and anxiety that may have gripped some staff members?

7. Was there a post-strategy in place to actively defend our market position against another competitive attack?

Within the framework of strengths and weaknesses, the following Sun Tzu statements are among those most often quoted:

In is according to the shapes that I lay the plans for victory, but the multitude does not comprehend this. Although everyone can see the outward aspects, none understand the way in which I have created victory.

Therefore, when I have won a victory, I do not repeat my tactics but respond to circumstances in an infinite variety of ways.

Now an organization may be likened to water. For just as flowing water avoids the heights and hastens to the lowlands, so an organization avoids strength and strikes weakness.

And as water shapes its flow in accordance with the ground, so an organization manages its victory in accordance with the situation of the competitor and the market.

And as water has no constant form, there are in the competitive marketplace no constant conditions.

Sun Tzu's comment that "an organization manages its victory in accordance with the situation" is totally relevant as many of today's organizations seek an agile and innovative work climate. In practice, such an organizational structure consists of two dimensions: physical and psychological.

Physical

Establishing a lean-and-mean, flexible, and, in current terms, agile organization has been an overriding goal in past decades. In part, the notion was to eliminate layers of management and any barriers that suggested a bureaucratic format, which would impede the free flow of upward and downward information.

Thus, the primary rationale for developing an organizational structure suited to the digital age is to create a work climate that invites creativity and innovation and which is free of cumbersome systems and procedures.

A prime example of such an approach is that taken by Dow Chemical (prior to its merger with DuPont.) The company attempted to reinvent itself by fostering a culture that takes on the character of a start-up.

Dow shifted from a traditional orientation of developing a portfolio of products to assembling a portfolio of value-added markets. That orientation is also expressed by how the organization has evolved from an inorganic chemical company, to an organic company, to a petrochemical company, to a plastics company.

Psychological

The psychological dimension of leading an agile organization leans heavily on the interaction between leaders and their staffs. It encompasses such all-embracing factors as morale and motivation, as well as the qualities of courage, determination, and persistence. Here is how one individual described a group leader:

"He was a very outstanding leader with calmness, consideration of all possibilities, and the courage to carry out his decision. He certainly set the example that had the respect of every individual in the group."

Likewise, those you manage want a self-confident leader who can accurately assess competitive and market conditions, and then motivate the staff to take decisive action. That capability is becoming increasingly more precise with the quantum leaps in digital technologies and artificial intelligence.

The endpoint is an organizational structure that can react where "there are in the competitive marketplace no constant conditions." The following two statements sum up Sun Tzu's theme on strengths and weaknesses.

One able to gain the victory by modifying his tactics in accordance with the rival's and market situation may be said to be extraordinary.

*Of the five elements, none is always predominant; of the four seasons, none lasts forever; of the days, some are long and some short, and the moon waxes and wanes.**

---

* Applicable to Sun Tzu's comment, and from another field of endeavor, the renowned sage, Rebbe Nachman of Breslov (1772-1810) said, "Each day has its own set of thoughts, words, and deeds. Live in tune."

10

Maneuver

Sun Tzu

Normally, when engaged for some major event, the leader first receives his direction from those at the highest level in the organization. He assembles the individuals directly involved and activates all those in support. He blends the entire group into a harmonious entity.

APPLICATIONS

Engaging an organization, or business group, "for some major event," such as entering a new market or preparing for a major product launch, entails an exacting process so that the leader "blends the entire group into a harmonious entity."

The process requires (1) a vision statement* with related strategic objectives, (2) an empowered cross-functional strategy team dedicated to the event, and (3) an agile organization displaying these attributes[†]:

- Quick to mobilize
- Nimble
- Collaborative
- Gets things done easily

---

* See Part 3 for guidelines on developing a vision statement.
[†] The attributes are based on McKinsey & Company's Organizational Health Index.

- Responsive
- Allows a free flow of information
- Quick at decision making
- Empowered to act
- Resilient
- Learns from failures

Sun Tzu continues:

> *Nothing is more difficult than the art of maneuver. What is difficult about maneuvers is making the devious route the most direct and turning misfortune to advantage.*
>
> *Thus, go by an indirect route and divert the rivals by enticing them with bait. So doing, you may set out after he does and arrive before him. One able to do this understands the strategy of the direct and the indirect.*

Sun Tzu previously introduced the concept of "indirect" in Chapter 2, "Developing Plans," where he stated that, "All confrontations are based on deception; and again in Chapter 9, "Energy," where he talked about normal and extraordinary forces.

Here, Sun Tzu refers to "direct and indirect" by using maneuver to gain an advantage. As in all of his references, the object is to avoid a direct, head-on confrontation where losses can be excessively high.

There is still a subtler interpretation of direct and indirect in the case of Eastman Kodak. Thinking its legendary name was protected by a renowned worldwide reputation and a solid public image, the company continued with a business-as-usual, direct approach.

Meanwhile, its overly confident executives lagged in switching to the industry-wide movement of digital photography. When Kodak's leadership finally responded to the change, it was too little, too late.

The once illustrious company subsequently declared bankruptcy. It eventually reorganized and downsized to a fraction of its original size, exited its primary markets, and moved in an entirely new direction.

The irony is that Kodak saw the coming of digital photography. It is even credited with inventing the digital camera in 1975. In the end, however, Kodak management remained focused on protecting its old technology and stoically watched as its market presence declined. The result: an industry that is identified with Kodak and a company that pioneered and popularized photography relinquished it to aggressive and forward-looking rivals.

One such rival, Fujifilm, chose an indirect maneuver. Its management watched a sharp drop in sales of its familiar green photo-film boxes and saw the distinct trend toward digital photography.

At that point, Fujifilm began an indirect maneuver around its photo-film roots to explore new science and technology markets. Examining its core competencies, company personnel found new ways to apply its technologies beyond film products. Result: Fujifilm moved into Ebola drugs, anti-aging lotions, and stem-cell research.

Sun Tzu now raises additional issues about maneuver:

Now both advantage and danger are inherent in maneuver.

One who sets the entire organization in motion to chase an advantage will not attain it.

Those who do not know the conditions of the market cannot conduct the movement.

Those who do not use local guides are unable to obtain the advantages of the ground.

He who knows the art of the direct and the indirect approach will be victorious. Such is the art of maneuvering.

Sun Tzu's general points of caution in the above statements apply directly to Fujifilm. Entering such diverse fields as anti-aging lotions and stem-cell research is subject to "both advantage and danger."

While the company sought to apply its core competencies in new fields, they faced physical obstacles and changing cultural influences, including new types of customers with distinct buying behaviors and new competitors with whom they had little or no experience. Thus, the three-step process described above is critical to avoiding "danger ... inherent in maneuver."

As for members of the strategy team, they faced a steep learning curve as they looked at target segments for points of entry. Also, "conditions of the market" meant getting individuals at the grass-roots level to a state of awareness, whereby they could alert the appropriate individuals to obstacles that could upend the marketing effort.

Sun Tzu continues with themes related to control and leadership:

> *Now an organization may be robbed of its spirits and its leader deprived of his courage.*
>
> *During the early morning spirits are keen, during the day they flag, and in the evening, thoughts turn toward home.*
>
> *In good order they await a disorderly rival; in serenity a clamorous one. This is control of the mental factor.*
>
> *Close to the contested place, they await a rival coming from afar; at rest, an exhausted rival; with well-trained personnel, eager ones. This is control of the physical factor.*

"An organization robbed of its spirits" relates to harmonious human relationships and reaching the hearts of your individuals. *Heart* collectively describes the emotional qualities by which you lead. These include unity, camaraderie, purpose, duty, and hope.

In day-to-day organizational life, emotions materialize in conflicting forms: order or confusion, commitment or indifference, boldness or fear, loyalty or deceitfulness. These, too, are the realities that typically dominate the heart.

Not only does heart underlie your role as a responsible manager, it is also reflected in your outward behavior and ability to perform as an inspiring leader. Consequently, a visible display of confidence, discipline, and purposeful direction filter down and impact your performance, and subsequently influence your capacity to manage your people and "control the human factor."

Thus, in all matters that pertain to an organization, it is the human heart that reigns supreme at the moment of crisis. Unfortunately, some managers rarely take it into account. And errors, sometimes irreversible, are the disastrous result.

Sun Tzu finalizes his discussion of the factors related to employing personnel with the following statements:

Therefore, the art of employing personnel is that when the rival occupies a commanding position, do not confront him; with his back resting on firm ground, do not oppose him.

When he pretends to flee, do not pursue.
  Do not attack his elite personnel.
  To a surrounded rival you must leave a way of escape.
  Do not press a rival at bay.
  This is the method of employing personnel.

11

The Nine Variables

Sun Tzu

There are some roads not to follow; some groups not to strike; some cities not to attack; and some ground which should not be contested.

Do not settle in low-lying ground.

In communicating ground, unite with your allies.

In isolated ground, do not linger.

In enclosed ground, resourcefulness is required.

In desperate ground, fight.

APPLICATIONS

If you substitute "ground" with "markets," there is a reasonable business parallel for reflecting on Sun Tzu's nine variables. Initially, it means going beyond the conventional approach of segmenting markets by demographic, geographic, and behavioral characteristics. Rather, you can use a comparative framework to sort through the advantages and disadvantages of markets, which leads to a more accurate assessment of those to avoid, defend, or fight for.

That framework consists of the following market categories, which consider Sun Tzu's nine variables: *natural, leading-edge, key, linked, central, challenging, difficult,* and *encircled.*

NATURAL MARKETS

Here, you operate in the familiar setting of ongoing established markets. The drawback is that within such customary surroundings, personnel tend to be at ease and are rarely motivated to venture out of their comfort zones. Yet, to expand, you must move beyond the confines of existing markets before the mature phase of the market life cycle sets in.

For the most part, in a natural market, you and your rivals have learned to adopt a live-and-let-live policy and thereby operate "in communicating ground." That condition exists as long as each company sticks to its own dedicated segment. Generally, outright aggressive confrontations are seldom used.

The primary reason for this uncharacteristic display of togetherness in a highly competitive world is that you and your rivals share a common interest in furthering the long-term growth and prosperity of the market.

LEADING-EDGE MARKETS

A leading-edge approach means exploring markets by making minor penetrations into a competitor's territory, with the aim of pursuing additional revenue streams. Such a move requires market intelligence to accurately determine the following:

- The investment needed to enter and gain a foothold in the market
- The feasibility of generating a revenue stream over the long term
- A timeframe for payback and eventual profitability
- An assessment of risks related to competitors' strengths and weaknesses

The previously mentioned case of Japanese companies entering North America with small copier machines in a market left open by Xerox illustrates this type of market. As for Xerox, it was a matter of lingering too long in "isolated ground."

KEY MARKETS

Within this category, you and many of your competitors seem evenly matched. The general behavior is that you would not intentionally create a conflict with an equally strong rival in "ground which should not be contested."

In some instances, however, you may find that a competitor is attempting to dislodge you from a long-held position with the clear aim of taking away customers or disrupting your supply-chain relationships. Then you may be forced to launch a counter-effort by concentrating resources to blunt the effort. Such actions are appropriate if they fit your overall strategic objectives.

LINKED MARKETS

In this market, you and your competitors have easy access to various segments. Your best strategy is to pay strict attention to constructing defensive barriers around those areas that you value most, and from which you can defend your position. In Sun Tzu's terms, it means, "in enclosed ground, resourcefulness is required."

Defensive barriers open to resourcefulness and inventiveness include strategies applied to:

- Product quality
- Product features and performance
- Customer service
- Technical support
- Pricing
- Warranties and guarantees
- Advanced technologies

Building such barriers should also result in strengthening customer relationships. You, thereby, benefit from a long-lasting, profit-generating advantage that is difficult for a competitor to overcome.

CENTRAL MARKETS

This relates to powerful forces that could threaten your market position. They are as diverse as watching competitors challenge your position through aggressive pricing, introducing dazzling new products, or announcing breakthrough technologies.

To counter such threats, look to joint ventures that would yield greater market advantages and offer more strategy options than you can achieve independently. For many companies, the merger and acquisition (M&A) route has proven the correct strategy to "unite with your allies."

CHALLENGING MARKETS

In this ground, if you enter a market dominated by a strong and aggressive competitor, be watchful. You could place your company at excessively high risk, as there are "some roads not to follow; some groups not to strike."

If, however, your long-term strategic objectives support maintaining a presence in a challenging market, then find a secure position, such as pinpointing an emerging or poorly served niche.

DIFFICULT MARKETS

This type of market is characterized as one where progress is erratic and highly competitive. That means, if you attempt to penetrate a market and secure key accounts, you are likely to be blocked.

In effect, you are trapped in an untenable situation and your entire plan could be in jeopardy. If your long-term strategic plan indicates remaining in the market, then your best course of action is to go forward. You are "in desperate ground, fight."

ENCIRCLED MARKETS

Encircled segments foretell a potentially risky situation. Any aggressive action by a stronger, well-positioned competitor can force you to consider pulling out of the market.

In such a situation, it is in your best interests to maintain ongoing competitor intelligence to assess the extent of your vulnerability. If, in your judgment, you lack the ability to mount a meaningful competitive response, then exiting the market is prudent, providing it minimizes disruption to your main business. The issue is that there are "some cities not to attack; and some ground which should not be contested."

Sun Tzu summarizes the above points:

> *A leader thoroughly versed in the advantages of the nine variable factors knows how to employ personnel.*
>
> *The leader who does not understand the advantages of the nine variables will not be able to use the ground to his advantage even though familiar with them.*
>
> *It is a doctrine of conflict not to assume the rival will not come, but rather to rely on one's readiness to meet him; not presume that he will not attack, but rather to make one's self invincible.*

Sun Tzu continues with a related theme tied to leadership.

> *There are five qualities which are dangerous in the character of a leader:*
> *If reckless, he can be defeated;*
> *If cowardly, he can be entrapped;*
> *If quick-tempered, he can be deceived;*
> *If too anxious to defend a reputation, he can be discredited;*
> *If an overly compassionate nature, he can be harassed.*
>
> *Now these five traits of character are serious faults in a leader and operations could be calamitous.*

What, then, are the positive leadership traits for today's digital age? There is no generally accepted list of traits that would satisfy most leaders. However, the following three sources characterize the most accepted characteristics:

First, "leadership is influencing people by providing purpose, direction, and motivation while operating to accomplish the mission and improve the organization."*

Second, from compiled lists, a manager's qualities include astuteness, straightforwardness, compassion, boldness, and strictness. (These are described in Chapter 5.)

Third, from a CEO of a high-tech organization: "To be a good leader, you have to have a vision. You have to have courage to go after it. And you have to have a reasonable track record of success. At the end of the day, you have to do what you think is right."

---

* Source: The U.S. Army Leadership Field Manual

12

Marches, Signals, Signs

Sun Tzu

When the rival is near, but lying low, he is depending on a favorable position.

When he aggressively challenges from afar, he wishes to lure you to advance; for when he is in easy ground he is in an advantageous position.

When many obstacles have been placed in the undergrowth, it is for the purpose of deception.

APPLICATIONS

The above statements are a sampling of conditions that Sun Tzu's army would have faced when crossing mountains, rivers, and rough terrain, and surmounting a variety of physical obstacles.

In everyday situations, "depending on a favorable position" means negotiating market terrain by means of a complex systems of logistics, concerns with weather, and use of technology (think drones and Amazon) in battling with competitors over the time it takes from customers placing orders to receiving their product.

In the following statements, Sun Tzu talks about signs that could indicate deep-rooted problems about leadership:

> *When personnel are disorderly, the leader has no prestige.*
>
> *If managers are short-tempered, they are exhausted.*
> *If rewards are too frequent, the leader is at the end of his resources; too frequent punishments that he is in acute distress.*
> *If leaders treat their staffs disrespectfully and later are fearful of them, the limit of discipline has been reached.*
>
> *When the rival's people are in high spirits, yet do not join battle for a long time, nor leave, you must thoroughly investigate the situation.*

In any of the above instances, the essential job is to identify troublesome signs and act before it explodes into an unrecoverable situation.

What types of market signals should alert you of an impending problem? Consider the following:

Competitors open or close regional offices or plants. There are sudden announcements of management changes. New layoffs are posted. Rumors persist of forthcoming competitive alliances that could unbalance marketplace practices.

Not to be overlooked are telltale signs of internal disorder and inept leadership as you observe competitors' personnel. For instance:

Managers openly show discouragement, display low morale, and exhibit short tempers, which could indicate that "the limit of discipline has been reached." Sales reps overtly look for other jobs, criticize working conditions, or complain about shortages of sales aids and supplies.

They whisper about ineffectual leadership and cuts in wages. They whine about stringent rules restricting travel-related expenses. Or they object to executives deliberately excusing (or overlooking) abuses in corporate procedures.

Then, there are other signals that may be harder to interpret, such as general disorder, sloppiness, or indications of internal desperation; or signs of changes in a competitor's traditional operating style, patterns in handling customer relationships, or the general attitude of executives in interacting with their personnel.

Other signals: Customers openly complain about the competitor's policies, rules, and procedures. And if you pump them for detailed information, they often surge forward with a flood of grievances.

Consider, too, the possible implications of the following market signals on your operation:

- A competitor abruptly announces a new value-added service. As importantly, the news triggers sudden interest among your customers.
- A competitor introduces generous financial incentives for distributors to aggressively push their products, and your customers show strong signs of responding to those incentives.
- Unforeseen promotional bursts from competitors siphon off sales that you counted on.
- A competitor suddenly shifts sales and service reps to a market segment that you thought was secure.
- An enhanced product, quietly and abruptly introduced by a competitor, suddenly stirs interest among your customers.
- An organizational shake-up at a key competitor indicates that a new leadership team is taking charge.

The significant point: It is in your best interests to red-flag significant market signals to "thoroughly investigate the situation." It is in such a state of unbalance and disarray that you can spot opportunities.

Sun Tzu sums up his statements with the following sage advice:

In conflict, numbers alone confer no advantage. Do not advance relying on sheer power.

It is sufficient to estimate the rival's situation correctly and to concentrate your strength against him. There is no more to it than this.

He who lacks foresight and underestimates his rival will surely be defeated by him.

If personnel are punished before their loyalty is secured, they will be disobedient. If not obedient, it is difficult to employ them.

If personnel are loyal, but punishments are not enforced, you cannot employ them.

Thus, command them with civility and imbue them uniformly with a fighting spirit and it may be said that victory is certain.

If orders which are consistently effective are used in instructing the troops, they will be obedient.
If orders which are not consistently effective are used in instructing them, they will be disobedient.
When orders are consistently trustworthy and observed, the relationship of a leader with his staff is satisfactory.

What does "command them with civility" mean? Any appropriate answer deals with the negatives and positives that exist in your organization. Although you may not be in a position to make changes, at least you can point to the instrument and push for change.

The following questions will help you personalize your own leadership style.

- Are priorities and objectives clearly stated and do your personnel generally accept them?
- Is there a system of recognition, rewards, and reprimands? Does it work?
- Do you seek input from subordinates? And do you act on the feedback provided? In particular, do you keep your people informed?
- In the absence of instructions, do individuals reporting to you have authority to make decisions that are consistent with your objectives?
- Are they empowered to act in times of opportunity or emergency?
- Are there signs of excessive tensions among employees, or acts of competitive in-fighting in the organization? What are the causes?
- Is your leadership style consistent with your company's values? Is there a working climate of trust? Do other leaders make positive or negative role models?

The following example illustrates these points:

Google, the online search giant, creates a working climate whereby its managers display the outstanding qualities of leadership by motivating their employees to innovate in all aspects of their jobs. Recognizing that inventiveness and innovation are the drivers of organizational success, its leadership is dedicated to creating a working culture that encourages fresh ideas.

For instance, Google management gives all engineers one day a week to develop their own pet projects, no matter how far from the company's central mission. If work deadlines get in the way of those free days for as much as a few weeks, they accumulate.

Also, the system is so pervasive that anyone at Google can post thoughts about new technologies or businesses on an *ideas* mailing list, available company-wide for inspection and input.

What are the leadership traits that support such behavior?

First, respect for the individual forms the basis of Google's leadership. In practice, it means recognizing and appreciating the inherent dignity and worth of people. And even where some individuals' ideas will not succeed, their efforts are recognized and respected. This is especially relevant when working with culturally diverse personnel with a wide range of ethnic and religious backgrounds.

Second, at each level, leaders stand aside and let subordinates do their jobs. They empower their people, give them tasks, delegate the necessary authority, and let them do the work.

The fundamental issue here is that the organization is not going to stop functioning because one leader steps aside. Therefore, central to the job of good leaders is helping subordinates grow and succeed by teaching, coaching, and counseling.

13

Terrain

Sun Tzu

Terrain which both we and the rival can cross with ease is called accessible. In such ground, he who first takes high positions convenient to his supply routes can compete advantageously.

Terrain easy to get out of but difficult to return to is entrapping. The nature of this ground is that if the rival is unprepared and you strike, you may defeat him. If the rival is prepared and you go out and engage, but do not win, it is difficult to return. This is unprofitable.

If I first occupy constricted ground, I must block the entry points and await the rival. If the rival first occupies such ground and blocks the routes, I should not follow him; if he does not block them completely, I may do so.

In precipitous ground, I must take a position on the high ground and await the rival. If he first occupies such ground, I lure him by leaving; I do not follow him.

When at a distance from a rival of equal strength, it is difficult to provoke a conflict and unprofitable to engage him in his chosen position.

These are the principles relating to six different types of terrain. It is the highest responsibility of the leader to inquire into them with the utmost care.

APPLICATIONS

The underlying significance of Sun Tzu's statements is that terrain—or, more precisely, markets—represents one of the fundamental factors in determining success and should be "the highest responsibility of the leader."

The evolving car-sharing business illustrates the difficulty of looking at the terrain under various market conditions. Consider Uber, Lyft, and Didi and how they used disruptive technologies to put the old-line taxi companies "in precipitous ground."

Even the traditional automotive companies, Toyota, Ford, General Motors, and BMW, tried to "take position on the high ground" in the evolving industry. They were followed by a new breed of disruptive competitors, Google and Tesla, that entered with their bold technologies and challenged the decades-old methods of making and powering vehicles. Still other companies focused on autonomous vehicles, as with the alliance of Uber and Toyota.

After losing customers, watching revenues nosedive, and even losing drivers to the startups, some taxi companies that initially did not "block the entry points" began fighting back to regain what they lost. They responded by outfitting their vehicles with electronic features, like those used by their new adversaries.

The essential point: Regaining a market position during periods of market turbulence goes beyond simply asking your staff for fresh ideas. And it certainly is outside the normal managerial practice of delegating.

Meaningful solutions from an empowered staff require them to interpret "terrain" and make reliable estimates and calculations about key issues before considering strategies and committing resources.

As a follow-on, Sun Tzu describes leadership issues related to marketplace conditions:

Now when personnel flee, are insubordinate, distressed, collapse in disorder or are routed, it is the fault of the leader. None of these disasters can be attributed to natural causes.

When troops are strong and leaders weak the organization is insubordinate.

When the leaders are valiant and personnel ineffective the organization is in distress.

When senior officers are angry and insubordinate, and on encountering the rival with no understanding of the feasibility of engaging, and without awaiting orders form the leader, the organization is in a state of collapse.

When the leader is morally weak and his discipline not strict, when his discipline not strict, when his instructions and guidance are not enlightened, when there are no consistent rules to guide the officers and men, and when the formation are slovenly, the organization is in disorder.

When a leader is unable to estimate his rival, uses a small force to engage a large one, or weak personnel to strike the strong, or when he fails to select superior staff, the result is route.

When any of these six conditions prevail, the organization is on the road to failure. It is the highest responsibility of the leader to examine them carefully.

The problems of a large communications company* matches some of the dysfunctional leadership issues described by Sun Tzu. The company pioneered a form of online communication that was wildly successful with a large, young population.

In a relatively short time, the inevitable occurred: Strong competition entered with essentially a copy of the originating company. Efforts to add features and create differentiation for the most part failed. And usage of

---

* The company is unnamed to prevent its embarrassment and for security reasons.

the service continued to decline, along with falling revenues, whereas competitors enjoyed continued growth.

Further, the company lost or replaced the heads of the engineering, finance, hardware, legal, product, and sales departments. Adding to the woes, investors in this public company becoming wary of the company being able to capitalize on its original innovation.

The turnaround: With the severe problems identified, the blame fell on the CEO for several reasons. Employees complained of dictatorial management and a penchant for secrecy, to the point of threatening jail time for employees who leaked proprietary information to the press.

At one point, employees were told they would not receive cash bonuses because the company didn't meet its goals. Yet, a survey revealed, they were not aware of what the goals were. Morale suffered.

The CEO fully acknowledged that "it is the highest responsibility of the leader to examine them carefully."

Sun Tzu continues by combining knowledge of the terrain with effective leadership with the following statements:

To estimate the rival's situation and to calculate distances and the degree of difficulty of the ground, so as to control victory, are virtues of the superior leader. He who fights with full knowledge of these factors is certain to win; he who does not will surely be defeated.

If the situation is one of victory, but the leader has issued orders not to engage, the manager may decide to fight. If the situation is such that he cannot win, but the leader has issued orders to engage, he need not do so.

And therefore, the leader who in advancing does not seek personal fame, and in withdrawing is not concerned with avoiding punishment, but whose only purpose is to protect the people and promote the best interest of the leader, is the precious jewel of the state.

Sun Tzu sums up the chapter by quantifying the chances of success:

If I know that my people are capable of striking the adversary, but do not know that he is invulnerable to attack, my chance of victory is but half.

If I know that the rival is vulnerable to attack, but do not know that my people are incapable of striking him, my chance of victory is but half.

If I know that the rival can be attacked and that my staff is capable of attacking them, but do not realize that because of the conditions of the ground I should not attack, my chance of victory is but half.

Therefore, when those experience in conflict move, they make no mistakes; when they act, their resources are limitless.

And therefore, I say: Know the rival, know yourself; you victory will never be endangered. Know the ground, know the weather; your victory will then be total.

14

The Variables of Ground*

Sun Tzu

Speed is the essence of conflict. Take advantage of the rival's unpreparedness; travel by unexpected routes, and strike where he has taken no precautions.

APPLICATIONS

From a leadership viewpoint, numerous conditions affect a firm where "speed is the essence of conflict." Referring again to Levi Strauss (see Chapter 7), the company faced severe problems.

Its design team was late in identifying key developments in fashion, such as colored denims for women and more tailored jeans for men. The situation was exacerbated as data revealed that females were the more frequent buyer of jeans, yet Levi had the smallest share of that lucrative buying group.

Then other internal problems surfaced, such as a lack of managerial discipline and an inability to correctly identify decisive points on which to concentrate, such as the female segment. Some senior-level executives, by their own admission, acted as if they had a monopoly on the denim market and gave little notice when young, fashion-conscious individuals began trading in their Levi's for more trendy styles offered by fast-moving rivals who could "strike where (Levi) has taken no precautions."

---

* Sun Tzu's original chapter begins by repeating the theme of the previous chapter on "Terrain." To avoid repetition, I open this chapter with his next topic, "Speed."

The essential points: Attempting to recover lost market share, competitive position, and customer loyalty are often costlier, more time consuming, and riskier than moving swiftly at the initial signs of declining sales.

Also, the failure to react rapidly often reaches deep into the organization, affecting product development and the ability to react with the appropriate products at the height of a sales cycle. Consequently, where there is ineffectual communications and the competence to turn market data into action, the cause can only be attributed to inept leadership.

Pay heed to nourishing personnel; do not unnecessarily fatigue them. Unite them in spirit; conserve their strength. Make unfathomable plans for the movements of the organization.

Fatigue is one of the characteristics that wears away at individuals' energies and results in an adverse effect on job performance, especially where extra levels of stamina and clear judgment are needed during times of market conflict.

Gauging the limits of fatigue is difficult. Yet you can get a reliable indication by listening carefully to individuals' comments and being attentive to their gestures.

These signs are especially noticeable among those who spend extensive periods of time traveling beyond their normal routines or where individuals do excessive amounts of overtime for long periods that can result in mental and physical wear-and-tear.

Thus, from a leader's point of view, how physical energy is expended should be a major concern. It matters most where it impacts staff morale, which could negatively affect the outcome of a campaign. That is, it makes the critical difference between success and failure, especially where a mindset is fragile and mood swings can deepen into depression.

Leaders who "pay heed to nourishing personnel" consider such variables as attitudes, morale, and physical and mental well-being. Remedies that organizations have used include providing employees with multiple weeks or months of paid sabbaticals, rewards in the form of periodic profit-sharing bonuses, and professional assistance in planning personal and professional goals.

There are other workable methods, such as helping individuals with finances; permitting participation in prestigious teams to develop new product ideas; allowing individuals greater freedom in making decisions that were previously reserved for more senior-level executives; or being selected to participate in special projects, such as improving travel and work schedules.

> *Throw the staff into a position from which there is no escape and even when faced with death, they will not flee. For if prepared to die, what can they not achieve? Then officers and men together put forth their utmost efforts.*
>
> *In a desperate situation they fear nothing; when there is no way out, they stand firm.*
>
> *Deep in a hostile land they are bound together, and there, where there is no alternative, they will engage the rival to the end.*

Being "Faced with death" is a metaphor for organizations that face severe reversals or bankruptcies. Once indomitable organizations, such as Levi Strauss, Eastman Kodak, and General Electric, suffered in this way. Levi eventually recovered, Kodak reorganized into a fraction of its former size, and General Electric (at the time of this writing) is attempting a turnaround.

Then, there were the US companies within the "rust belt" that stumbled, which had a devastating effect on the economic well-being of cities, towns, and communities as it crushed the livelihoods of tens of thousands of families.

Therefore, it is fair to speculate about what would have occurred if "officers and men together put forth their utmost efforts."

One answer is illustrated by Opel, which experienced heavy losses when owned by General Motors. After severing relationships and moving to new ownership from the makers of Peugeot and Citroen vehicles, it quickly turned profitable. A new CEO made peace with once-skeptical unions, and "officers and men," working together, figured out how to profitably produce low-margin cars in a high-cost country.

Another answer comes from Chapter 1 and is worth repeating:

> *"Relying on oneself to make rational decisions can be overwhelming and often counter-productive. Whereas actively embracing*

> empowerment as a primary requirement of leadership improves your chances of making accurate decisions. When people are empowered with freedom of speech and thought, their minds tend to be flexible and inventive."
>
> Thus, such individuals need no encouragement to be vigilant. Without forcing their support, the leader obtains it; without inviting their affection, he gains it; without demanding their trust, he wins it.
>
> To cultivate a uniform level of valor is the object of the administration. And it is by proper use of the ground that weak and strong personnel are used to the best advantage.

"Proper use of the ground" is particularly applicable to a sales territory or market segment. It is reasonable to assume that some salespeople and their managers, consciously or not, consider the long and short-term economic outlook of their respective territories.

They think about the actions of competitors and how to respond to their strategies and tactics. They watch for changes in buyer behavior that would define the direction of the market, and subsequently consider what feedback to offer about changes in the product and service mix.

Consequently, where members of the salesforce can think strategically, where each would act as if general manager of their respective territories, then it would help to "cultivate a uniform level of valor," whereby "individuals need no encouragement to be vigilant."

To that end, see Part 3 for guidelines to developing a Strategic Business Plan to assist all those working at the grass-roots level, in particular the sales staff, to think like strategists.

Sun Tzu moves on with the following statements:

> He should be capable of keeping his officers and men in ignorance of his plans.
>
> He prohibits practices and so rids the staff of doubts. Then, until the right moment, there can be no troubles.

He changes his methods and alters his plans, so that people have no knowledge of what he is doing.

He makes it impossible for others to anticipate his purpose.

The above statements would seem to contradict my previous commentary on empowerment and staff planning. Not so. Market conditions could dictate a prudent for-your-eyes-only approach, where some layers of staff would be left in the dark for a period.

This is especially the case where secrets of a technology breakthrough would inadvertently leak to competitors, or in situations where surprise is the centerpiece of a product-launch strategy.

Sun Tzu summarizes with the following statement:

Set personnel to their tasks without imparting your designs; use them to gain advantage without revealing dangers involved. Throw them into a perilous situation and they survive; put them in death ground and they will live.

For when the organization is placed in such a situation it can snatch victory from defeat.

15

Attack

APPLICATIONS

Sun Tzu's statements correspond to tactical maneuvers, which are short-term actions to achieve short-term objectives. And if used correctly, they support longer-term strategic objectives.

"Fire to assist their attacks" relates to the components of the marketing mix* when used in market campaigns for "different fire-attack situations."

When formed into a comprehensive plan, where the aim is to satisfy customers' technical and service needs as well as to counter threats from rivals, it equates to "those who use barrages."

Thus, the make-up of the tactical plans that form "barrages" is likely to focus on specific objectives, such as:

- Maximize the effectiveness of the salesforce
- Improve relationships along the supply chain

---

* The marketing mix, also referred to as the 4Ps, is generally understood to include product, price, promotion, and place (distribution).

- Secure a defensible market position against aggressive competitors
- Launch a new product and generate demand in target segments
- Build familiarity and easy recognition of a company or brand
- Neutralize a competitor's efforts by countering false or inaccurate claims
- Interact with customers to solve their problem and thereby strengthen connections

Now to win campaigns and take your objectives, but to fail to exploit these achievements is troubling and may be described as wasteful delay.

In a digital world where decisiveness, action, and surprise are ingredients leading to successful outcomes, Sun Tzu's comment is an insightful affirmation for using speed to "win campaigns and take your objectives."

Noteworthy firms that have embraced speed to "exploit ... achievement" include the likes of Facebook, Amazon, and Alphabet. Conversely, few firms have succeeded by delaying action, especially when operating in a highly competitive marketplace, as did Kodak and Levi Strauss, referred to in previous chapters.

Procrastination, therefore, is outright dangerous and contrary to what data analytics is supposed to accomplish. Yet, the reality does exist that too many firms are burdened with imbedded organizational issues, such as a sluggish corporate culture that tolerates drawn-out deliberations, cumbersome committees, long chains of command, and a general malaise whereby indecisiveness stalls action.

Notwithstanding today's movement toward empowerment, built-in delays exist, as documented in a survey of over 23,000 employers that report "60 percent of personnel must consult with at least 10 colleagues each day just to get their jobs done."

As a result, those organizations don't benefit from what big data has to offer. Moreover, from a leadership point of view, there is the potential damage that prolonged efforts have on staff morale. Result: Interest is often diverted, enthusiasm is erased, and any value from positive expectancy is lost.

And should the insidious effects of complacency creep in, alert competitors would take advantage of the "wasteful delay" to exploit the opportunity.

Therefore, it is said that enlightened leaders deliberate upon the plans, and good leaders execute them.

If not in the interests of the organization, do not act. If you cannot succeed, do not use personnel. If you are not in danger, do not fight.

Sun Tzu divides the responsibilities of individuals "deliberating on plans" from those who "execute them." The late President Dwight D. Eisenhower expressed the concept thus: "the plan is nothing; planning is everything." His comment is generally understood to mean that any plan on paper is stagnant; there must be action components consisting of strategies and tactics that result in tangible outcomes.

As for the "interests of the organization," this guideline is decided by the firm's vision.*

Sun Tzu summarizes by describing the characteristics of a leader.

A leader cannot organize a group because he is enraged, nor can one fight because he is resentful. For while an angered man may again be happy, and a resentful man again be pleased, an organization that has perished cannot be restored.

Therefore, the open-minded leader is prudent, and the good manager is warned against rash action. Thus, the state is kept secure and the staff safeguarded.

For your purposes and within the framework of Sun Tzu's reference to an "open-minded leader," there are tangible characteristics that define today's successful leaders.† In general, it is the inquiring rather than the creative mind, the comprehensive rather than the specialized approach, the calm rather than the excitable head, the flexible rather than the stubborn attitude, the determined rather than the indecisive personality that can sustain self-confidence and lead.

---

* See Appendix for a full description of the importance of a corporate vision with guidelines on how to develop a vision statement.
† The previous chapters also include references, comments, and guidelines about effective leadership.

As for your role as a leader: You must connect with your staff. This can be challenging, especially where most individuals arrive with a set of built-in values, developed and nurtured from childhood through lifetime experiences. In varying degrees, these values are expressed as loyalty, duty, respect, and integrity.

However, these can also be empty ideals and may not fully surface if your personal behavior does not mesh with your organization's values, ethics, rules, and culture. Where an interconnect occurs through words, deeds, and everyday practice, you must communicate purpose, provide direction, and instill motivation. Once again, it starts with a corporate or business unit vision.

Where empowerment is accepted as corporate policy, what characteristics should you be looking for in a potential leader?

First and foremost, and as indicated above, you want a self-confident individual who can accurately assess competitive conditions. That person should then be able to utilize big data and convert it into smart data that gives clarity about what needs to be accomplished. And that person must be able to direct, motivate, and develop skills in others, so that they can act.

For instance:

Direction means prioritizing tasks, assigning responsibility for completing them, and making sure personnel understand the organization's vision. The aim is also to deploy resources for the best outcome.

Motivation inspires personnel to act on their own initiative when they see something that needs to be done—that is, within the overall guidelines of business objectives.

Skills relate to the technical competence to use required tools and techniques. Skills also pertain to understanding how to work within the new frontiers of digital technology and their known and yet-to-be-discovered applications.

Action means assessing the market and competitive situation, looking for opportunities, developing strategies and tactical plans, and implementing them.

The endpoint is that "the state (organization) is kept secure and the staff safeguarded."

16

Employment of Secret Agents

> **Sun Tzu**
>
> *One who confronts his rival for many years to struggle for victory in a decisive campaign, yet who, because he begrudges rank, honors, and financial rewards, remains ignorant of his rival's situation, is completely devoid of humanity. Such a man is no leader; no support of his organization; no master of victory.*
>
> *Now the reason the enlightened leader wins over the rival whenever they move, and their achievements surpass those of ordinary men, is foreknowledge.*

APPLICATIONS

Market intelligence is "foreknowledge." Using it wisely forms the underpinnings of virtually all competitive strategy. It improves your ability to sort through data analytics to pinpoint a competitor's strengths and weaknesses and thereby allocate resources with greater precision.

And depending on the accuracy of the intelligence, the predictive analytics indicates a new product's acceptance among customers before a full-scale introduction campaign gets underway. It is then possible that your "achievements surpass those of ordinary men."

What is called foreknowledge cannot be elicited from spirits, nor by analogy with past events, nor from calculations. It must be obtained from men who know the rival's situation.

"Men who know the rival's situation" translates to those individuals who are effective at assembling information through personal interaction and observation. They would screen and interpret events and news and authenticate information that comes in from various sources. They are also useful in exploring the human side of competitive intelligence and reporting the behaviors and personalities of key individuals.

However, before selecting prospective agents, you want to find out their special skills, and, most importantly, why they want to undertake such a task. Once you know their motivation, you can determine how best to employ them.

Some individuals are only interested in money, with little concern for obtaining accurate information about the competitor's true situation. In such cases, question their integrity and use great care in using them. Also, be sure to communicate clearly the specific information you need.

Now there are five sorts of secret agents to be employed. These are native, inside, doubled, expendable, and living.

When these five types of agents are all working simultaneously, and none knows their method of operation, they are called the treasure of a leader.

Native agents are those of the rival's staff whom we employ.

"Native agents" are especially effective when networking with key individuals during professional gatherings. Such venues are where people tend to freely share their company's information through informal conversations or through keynote presentations.

They are somewhat uncaring about their respective company's security, or their desire for recognition makes them oblivious to the dangers of revealing company secrets.

They listen in when noteworthy executives present technical papers at open meetings, which often detail sensitive information about their company's upcoming products, services, and even market-entry plans. And at the question-and-answer period, the speaker, trying further to impress an audience, inadvertently pours out more confidential data.

Another prime time for intelligence gathering is the familiar hospitality suite where alcohol and talk flow easily. It is a spot where security is often lax, and everyone's guard is down.

Inside agents are rival officials whom we employ.

"Inside agents" may have been bypassed for promotion, feel underpaid and underappreciated, are relegated to insignificant jobs, or are generally pushed aside in a variety of political or power struggles within the organization.

They feel abused and see their careers languishing unless they make some bold move. They may also find themselves surrendering to financial pressures to keep family and self whole. And their attitude may be "now or never."

You need to assess such individuals carefully for their stability and determine how to use them judiciously. Obviously, you want their information, within the bounds of ethical and legal guidelines.

Beyond personal observations, you would employ inside agents for their expertise in obtaining meaningful information from scientific and professional journals, industry studies, product literature, or innovative projects described in articles and professional papers written by the competitors' employees.

Doubled agents are rival agents whom we employ.

These "doubled agents" may try to extract intelligence about your company. Stay alert to their intentions. Once identified, you could attempt to turn them around and get them working on your behalf.

They would then serve in the same capacity as inside agents. Here, too, you can assume that doubled agents seek lavish rewards. However, it is in your best interests to exercise caution.

Determine the veracity of these individuals, the reliability of their information, and how long you can expect them to remain loyal to your cause. Once again, make certain you are not violating your company's ethical, legal, or policy guidelines.

> *Expendable agents are those of our own people who are deliberately given fabricated information.*

These "expendable agents" are your own people who are deliberately fed inaccurate information, which is disseminated in a variety of ways to cause competitors to make wrong decisions. These contrived leaks take many forms.

For example, it could involve passing fabricated information about new product features, prices, and delivery schedules through sales reps who meet competitors' reps. Or it could be executives revealing false dates about a product launch that would disrupt a competitor's plans.

Despite your possible discomfort when undertaking such activities, look at the situation strictly from a strategist's viewpoint. Misinformation needs distribution to divert competitors from directly opposing your strategy moves.

You thereby preserve your company's hard-won market position, control needless expenditures of financial and human resources fighting unnecessary market battles, and avoid disrupting your strategies.

> *Living agents are those who return with information.*

These "living agents" usually provide the most credible information. They are generally experienced, talented, and loyal individuals who can gain access to, and become intimate with, a competitor's high-level executives. They sit in a position to learn their plans and observe their movements. These individuals are truly the eyes and ears of a company and often enjoy the closest and most confidential relationships.

Perhaps the one unsettling issue to cope with when using agents—but certainly worth knowing—is which of your employees intentionally or inadvertently passes on your company's information directly or indirectly to competitors. Eventually, those individuals are exposed, and you can obtain valuable clues about what motivated them to those acts.

Another concern: Engaging in such stealth activities is usually contrary to the type of practices most managers care to undertake. Again, think of business intelligence as essential to running a company in a highly competitive environment. Above all, it is indispensable to the development and integrity of competitive strategies.

Sun Tzu summarizes with the following sage advice:

> *Generally, in the case of rivals you wish to strike, territories you wish to occupy, and people you wish to target, you must know the names of the rival leaders, the staff officers, and other key personnel. You must instruct your agents to inquire into these matters in minute detail.*

> *And therefore, only the enlightened leader who can use the most intelligent people as agents is certain to achieve great things. Secret operations are essential in conflict; upon them the organization relies to make its every move.*

Part 2

Carl von Clausewitz

OVERVIEW

Carl von Clausewitz is regarded as one of the greatest Western military thinkers. His book *On War*, published posthumously by his widow in 1832, is considered by many eminent scholars as the most distinguished Western work on war ever written.

On War has influenced generations of soldiers, statesmen, historians, and intellectuals throughout the world—and it is still being studied today at most military academies.

Clausewitz, a Prussian soldier and writer, was born in 1780. He first encountered war in 1793 as a 13-year-old infantry ensign. During the Jena campaign, he was captured, and while in service with the Russians, he played a prominent part in the Moscow campaigns of 1812–1813.

On rejoining the Prussian service, he became chief of staff and later director of the Military Academy in Berlin. There, he attracted the attention of the distinguished General Scharnhorst, whom he later helped to reform the Prussian army.

More than a soldier, Clausewitz was a philosopher. It is in this framework that he recognized war as a political phenomenon. Consequently, if conflict was meant to achieve a political purpose, everything that entered into war—social and economic preparation, strategic planning, the conduct of operations, and the use of force on all levels—should be determined by this purpose.

The following is a sampling of Clausewitz's more dynamic concepts from each of the following chapters:

- *In conflict, even the ultimate outcome is never to be regarded as final. The outcome is merely a transitory evil, for which a remedy may still be found in a variety of possible conditions at some later date.*
- *The opponent's capabilities must be neutralized; that is, they must be put in such a condition that they can no longer carry on the conflict.*
- *If we ask what sort of mind is likeliest to display the qualities of genius, it is the inquiring, rather than the creative mind, the comprehensive rather than the specialized approach, the calm rather than the excitable head to which we entrust the fate of our personnel, and the safety and honor of our organization.*
- *Action in conflict is like movement in a resistant element. Just as the simplest movement, walking, cannot easily be performed in water, so in conflict it is difficult for normal efforts to achieve even moderate results.*
- *Rather than comparing conflict to art, we could more accurately compare it to commerce, which is also a conflict of human interests and activities.*
- *Just as a businessman cannot take the profit from a single transaction and put it into a separate account, so an isolated advantage gained in conflict cannot be assessed separately from the overall result.*
- *Conflicts consist of a large number of engagements, great and small, simultaneous or consecutive. Each of these has a specific purpose relating to the whole.*

- *We maintain unequivocally that the form of confrontation that we call defense offers greater probability of victory than attack.*
- *A leader must never expect to move on the narrow ground of imagined security and feel that the means he is using are the only ones possible—and persist in using them even at the thought of their possible inadequacy.*
- *What matters is to detect the culminating point of actions with discriminative judgment.*
- *Two basic principles underlie all strategic planning: First, act with the utmost concentration; second, act with the utmost speed.*

17

What Is Conflict

Clausewitz

To secure an objective, we must render the rival powerless; and that is the true aim of conflict.

To introduce moderation into conflict would always lead to logical absurdity.

If you want to overcome your opponent, you must match your effort against his power of resistance.

APPLICATIONS

Clausewitz likens conflict to a duel, with one trying to overcome the other, or submit to his will, but only on a larger scale. The core idea is to make the rival incapable of further resistance.

The metaphor is plausible and applicable for various types of competitive confrontations in the everyday marketplace. Consider, for instance, a company that mounts a strong resistance to retain its existing market position.

Or think of the organization that penetrates a market already occupied by a strong competitor. Yet those defenders have no notion of relinquishing their dominant position without a fight.

Then, there are instances where defenders "introduce moderation into conflict" as their way of protecting a market position. They erroneously rely on a distinguished market history and a strong public image.

Many of those once proud enterprises were left in shambles. Others were forced to exit their primary markets or go through a massive downsizing, as in the cases of Eastman Kodak and General Electric (referenced in Parts 1 and 2).

The essential point: To counter any threat to your position, "you must match your effort against his power of resistance," with the aim of blunting the rival's advantage. That also means assessing the resources at his or her disposal and the strength of his or her will. You, thereby, become a threat to him or her as much as he or she is a threat to you.

> *In conflict, even the ultimate outcome is never to be regarded as final.*
>
> *The outcome is merely a transitory evil, for which a remedy may still be found in a variety of possible conditions at some later date.*

The central idea underlying Clausewitz's statement is that an encounter with a rival should not be viewed as an isolated incident. Rather, it is part of a continuum, consisting of several successive campaigns, so that the outcome of each campaign determines the strategy for the one that follows.

Once your staff internalizes that "the (negative) outcome is merely a transitory evil," and "a remedy may still be found," they can draw on the intrinsic power of their minds to reimagine new strategies. Here is where your leadership is needed to enable empowerment and use it as the mechanism to stretch their thinking to fashion new possibilities. The process begins by providing personnel with purpose and direction, which are encased in a vision.*

Acting on this point has huge ramifications for you, and any leader. If left unattended, the human tendency is to fall back and accept failure.

Worse yet, the inclination is for some individuals to drop into a state of despair, which would have severe repercussions for employee morale. Such feelings of hopelessness could spread throughout the organization or business unit.

---

* See Part 3 on how to develop a vision statement.

However modest the leader's demands may be, however small the resources employed, and however limited the objective, once an effort is under way, actions cannot be interrupted even for a moment.

Every action needs a certain time to be completed. That period is called its duration, and length will depend on the speed at which individuals work.

Whereas Clausewitz recognized the differences in individuals and their innate capabilities for completing a task, the realities of today's competitive world dictate some remedies. The obvious ones include pairing individuals to complement each other's capabilities, assigning the appropriate task to an individual who matches the skillset needed to do the job, and providing the proper work environment.

Then, there is the issue of leadership and discipline. Preparing your staff to bear up under intense competitive conditions involves a good deal of leadership skill. This is particularly essential when individuals are naturally predisposed to back away from the realities of an uncertain and erratic competitive threat.

Therefore, your aim is to motivate individuals to make audacious efforts to reverse a situation and turn potential defeat into victory. Clausewitz's sage advice again holds true: "in conflict even the ultimate outcome is never to be regarded as final."

Accordingly, tune in to what psychological effects competitive conditions have on your employees. Your central task, therefore, is to inspire individuals by reinforcing the idea that there are always actions that can change dire conditions into successful outcomes.

The central point: If handled skillfully, you can reignite your staff's creativity and energy to find solutions to a supposed untenable situation. How effectively you handle this task goes a long way to determining how your subordinates judge you as a manager.

A factor that can bring action to a standstill: imperfect knowledge of the situation.

In his writings, Clausewitz makes the additional point that the only situation a leader can know with any reliability is his own; he can know his competitor's only from unreliable intelligence.

Notwithstanding today's increasing availability of big data, algorithms, and analytics, you still must examine incoming intelligence for accuracy, determine its application, and check on when it was collected, by whom, and with what systems. With such variables, "imperfect knowledge of the situation" is a distinct reality.

Thus, even a minor mistake can lead you to suppose that the initiative lies with your competitor when in fact it remains with you. Or an incorrect estimate could rank your rival's strength too high, rather than too low. Clausewitz asserts further that absolute, so-called mathematical factors never find a firm basis in all calculations.

Still, all is not lost. If you thoughtfully observe patterns of competitive behavior, you can arrive at some level of accuracy about what to expect. Admittedly, changes in psychological and behavioral attitudes are difficult to interpret. Yet it can be done by carefully watching how a competitor reacts to your own actions. For instance, such telltale signs include noticing the speed of reaction to a pricing change or a sudden promotional incentive, estimating the levels of commitment made in personnel and other resources, or observing which actions are acted on and those that receive little or no response.

> *Only the element of chance is needed to make conflict a gamble, and that element is never absent.*

As previously mentioned, even with all the sophisticated methodologies and absolute claims associated with the providers of analytics, there is still the unpredictability of human behavior spiraling in a maelstrom of internal and external forces. Or as Clausewitz states, "there is interplay of possibilities, probabilities, good luck and bad" during the entire period a campaign is active.

These dynamics at play, in turn, form the foundations of chance, which continually vibrates in every conflict, as documented by the success rate of new product launches at 50%.

Clausewitz sums up his chapter on conflict with the following statements:

Conflict is an act of policy based on its strategic direction ... and should never be an isolated incident.

Conflict never breaks out wholly unexpectedly; nor can it be spread instantaneously. Each side can therefore gauge the other to a large extent by what he is and does.

The strategic objective—the original motive for the conflict—will determine both the objective to be reached and the amount of effort it requires.

18

Purpose and Means in Competitive Conflict

> **Clausewitz**
>
> *The opponent's capabilities must be neutralized; it must be put in such a condition that its personnel can no longer carry on the conflict. All plans are ultimately based on it.*
>
> *To make the adversary fear for the final outcome can be considered as a shortcut to a successful conclusion.*

APPLICATIONS

Clausewitz's concept that "the opponent's capabilities must be neutralized" has its business applications through the following maneuvers.

First, look for ways to apply your strengths against a competitor's weaknesses. The essence of the move is that you position your resources so that your rival cannot, will not, or simply lacks the capability and spirit to challenge your efforts.

Second, focus greater attention toward serving customers' needs and resolving their problems in a manner that visibly outperforms your competitors.

Third, search for a psychological advantage by creating an unbalancing effect in the rival manager's mind, whereby he or she hesitates in indecision. The aim is to disorient and unbalance the competing manager into wasting time and making irreversible mistakes.

Fourth, attempt to hold a long-term position in a target market, as gauged by attaining a market share objective, securing a position on the supply train, reaching a profitability goal, or similar metrics.

One aggressive company illustrated some of the above points when it maneuvered to gain an advantage over an established organization in a specialized market. Such is the case with a mobile payments company, Square, which enables small businesses, from local hardware stores to restaurants, to accept credit card payments via a small plastic reader that attaches to a smartphone.

In one year, the St. Louis, MO firm processed $15 billion in transactions, up from $5 billion during the previous 12-month period. Not unexpectedly, Square was being watched by a strong, deep-pocketed competitor, Intuit. The rival serves a substantial customer base of five million small businesses with its popular QuickBooks. It, too, sells a Square-like credit reader called GoPayment.

Square founder Jack Dorsey claims that his approach to reducing the opponent's effectiveness sits in a line of attack that his rival cannot claim: an ability to get people to come together behind him, to believe in his vision, and to buy into the cool image that Square has managed to develop.

The central issues: Will such an advantage be powerful enough to increase Square's market share? Is the advantage sustainable enough to spearhead an ongoing offensive and secure a sizeable market penetration?

The sustainable part, however, will be determined at some later time, depending first, on when and how Intuit decides to react; and second, on the durability of Dorsey's strategy to "to make the adversary fear for the final outcome."

Clausewitz continues with his theme of neutralizing the opponent with the following statements:

Make the conflict costlier for the opponent by wasting his human, material, and financial resources.

Resistance is a form of action, aimed at reducing enough of the rival's power to force him to abandon his intentions.

If a mere presence is enough to cause the opponent to abandon his position, the objective has been achieved.

If we wish to gain total victory, then the weakening of the opponent's capabilities is the most appropriate action; to seize a dominant position is only a consequence.

In competitive situations, many paths lead to success. They range from causing the rival to waste its resources and "make the conflict costlier," losing a dominant market position, to waiting for the "opponent to abandon his position." Any one of these may be used to overcome the opponent's will.

In some instances, wearing down the opponent means waiting passively. To be totally effective, however, that strategy must contain proactive components.

For example, consider the following approaches, which could contribute to "weakening of the opponent's capabilities."

- Pursue revenue-expansion opportunities as well as cost-reduction approaches. By latching on to new systems and digital technologies, it is possible to create a meaningful competitive advantage, and thereby neutralize the opponent's capabilities.
- Position yourself in the market through rapid maneuvers, so that the competitor cannot anticipate your moves in sufficient time to counter your actions with a meaningful defense.
- Focus your resources on an emerging, neglected, or poorly served market. Your aim is to avoid a direct, head-on confrontation with a stronger rival. An alternative aim is to cause the competitor to haphazardly spread resources by incorrectly anticipating your direction, thereby further weakening his or her primary efforts.
- Create a differentiated product, or value-added service, that is not easily cloned.
- Develop a system that provides accurate market intelligence so that you can take fast action against market opportunities and, as importantly, that allows you to react quickly to any areas of a competitor's vulnerabilities.
- Initiate constructive relationships with customers that lock out competitors for an extended sales cycle.

Electrolux, the Swedish appliance maker, exhibited several of these approaches when it tried to overtake its chief rivals, Whirlpool and Haier, in areas where the company was experiencing brutal price competition.

Electrolux's primary strategy was to create a differentiated product. It began by sending market researchers into customers' homes where they spent hours observing and questioning people about their vacuum cleaners. They were especially anxious to find out about problems they were encountering.

The resulting market intelligence led Electrolux to develop a bagless vacuum cleaner. Bringing together the design, research and development, and marketing departments, the combined group came up with a product that used a unique technology to compress dust into a spongy pellet, thereby eliminating any irritating and harmful dust circulating in the air.

> *Our discussion has shown that while many different roads can lead to the attainment of the strategic objective, confrontation is the only possible means. Everything is governed by a supreme law, the decision by force.*

"The decision by force" is regarded by many as one of Clausewitz's most famous concepts. Yet, that phrase is fraught with contradictions, which could lead to false interpretations.

For instance, in other parts of his writings, he states,

> *The fact that engagements do not always aim at blunting the rival's efforts, their objectives can often be attained without any confrontation at all, but merely by an evaluation of the situation. That explains why entire campaigns can be conducted with great energy, even though actual confrontation plays an unimportant part in them.*

Clausewitz goes on to say,

The leader may exploit any weaknesses in the opponent's capabilities and strategy and finally reach a peaceful settlement. If his assumptions are sound and promise success, we are not entitled to criticize him.

In another time and space, with almost 2,500 years separating Clausewitz from Sun Tzu, the Chinese general wrote, "To win one hundred victories in one hundred battles is not the acme of skill. To subdue the enemy without fighting is the acme of skill."*

Clausewitz ends the chapter with the following statements that sum up purpose and means in competitive conflict.

Preserving our own forces amounts to pure resistance, whose ultimate aim can only be to prolong the conflict until the rival is exhausted.

When we speak of reducing the opponent's forces we must emphasize that nothing obliges us to limit this idea to physical forces. The morale element must also be considered.

---

* Scholars generally agree that Clausewitz never read Sun Tzu, *The Art of War.*

19

On Genius

Clausewitz

We often see that the most intelligent people are indecisive. Since in the rush of events a man is governed by feelings rather than by thought, the intellect needs to arouse the quality of courage, which then supports and sustains it in action.

Looked at in this way, the role of determination is to limit the agonies of doubt and the perils of hesitation when the motives for action are inadequate.

We believe that determination proceeds from a special type of mind, from a strong rather than a brilliant one. There are many examples of men who show great determination at the junior levels, but lose it as they rise in rank. Conscious of the need to be decisive, they also recognize the risks entailed by a wrong decision.

APPLICATIONS

Clausewitz's emphasis on determination is supported by the following cross-section of famous personalities:

"A dream doesn't become reality through magic; it takes sweat, determination and hard work." Colin Powell

"I never could have done what I have done without the habits of punctuality, order, and diligence, without the determination to concentrate myself on one subject at a time." Charles Dickens

"Not only our future economic soundness but the very soundness of our democratic institutions depends on the determination of our government to give employment to idle men." Franklin D. Roosevelt

"The truest wisdom is a resolute determination." Napoleon Bonaparte

"Let us not be content to wait and see what will happen, but give us the determination to make the right things happen." Horace Mann

"If your determination is fixed, I do not counsel you to despair. Few things are impossible to diligence and skill. Great works are performed not by strength, but perseverance." Samuel Johnson

Four elements make up the climate of competitive encounters: danger, exertion, uncertainty, and chance. If we consider them together, it becomes evident how much fortitude of mind and character is needed to make progress in these impeding elements with safety and success.

Such are the burdens that the leader's courage and strength of will must overcome, if he hopes to achieve outstanding success. The burdens increase with the number of men in his command, and therefore the higher his position is, the greater the strength of character he needs to bear the mounting load.

Clausewitz covers diverse points in his views on "mind and character" and "the burdens that the leader's courage and strength of will must overcome." For you, the following generally accepted guidelines can provide a measure of relief from some of those burdens:

- Hold fast to the definitive object of all businesses, which, according to the late management scholar Peter Drucker, is to "create a customer."
- Remove obstacles that prevent your people from providing quality of service and delivering innovative products.
- Establish cross-functional teams of workers to actively engage their thinking and tap into their creativity, then listen to them.

- Introduce a work environment built around empowerment, which reaches beyond job title or position, so that individuals of all ranks can assume the enhanced role of leader.
- Commit to long-term goals, such as developing leading-edge products or maintaining superior service and product quality.
- Eliminate the use of fear as a motivator. Rather, inspire others by focusing on the realization of the corporate or business-unit vision.
- Institute continuing employee training and education around the five pillars that define the digital-age organization: vision, empowerment, influence, strategy excellence, and corporate culture.

Of all the passions that inspire men in conflict, none is so powerful and so constant as the longing for honor and renown. Other emotions may be more common and more venerated—loyalty, idealism, enthusiasm—but they are no substitute for a thirst for fame and honor.

They may rouse the mass to action and inspire it, but they cannot give the leader the ambition to strive higher than the rest, as he must if he is to distinguish himself.

And so far as a leader is concerned, we may well ask whether history has even known a great leader who was not ambitious— whether such a figure is conceivable.

Clausewitz talks about two issues: "the longing for honor and renown" and "the ambition to strive higher than the rest."

First, honors: The seemingly unquenchable desire for awards continues in the form of certificates, prizes, and plaques that recognize individuals by accomplishment, by industry, by age, by outstanding leader, and so on.

Psychologists have shown that people often value status above and beyond monetary rewards. It reaches the point where such individuals are even willing to incur their own costs to buy high status. The object of these yearnings is to satisfy the need for social status, image, and reputation.

Thus, the quest for positive recognition is a characteristic Clausewitz emphasizes as "a thirst for fame and honor."

Second, ambition: Clausewitz raises the question "whether history has ever known a great leader who was not ambitious—whether such a figure is conceivable."

Ambition is generally accepted as a quality that exists among most leaders. However, for practical application, ambition should be worthy of the organization's vision and not a pathway to personal power.

From another viewpoint, ambition is difficult to separate from courage. In thinking about outstanding leaders, it is challenging to decide which of their actions in the face of severe problems bore the mark of boldness or that of ambition. Both are characteristics of the truly outstanding leader.

Constructive ambition stimulates ambition in others. It arouses determination, which gives momentum to the organization. Thus, nurturing positive ambition in others is an essential duty of the leader, especially where empowerment exits:

> *A strong character is one that will not be unbalanced by the most powerful emotions; that is, if we consider how men differ in their emotional reactions. For instance:*
>
> *First, we find a group with small capacity for being roused, usually known as unemotional or calm.*
>
> *Second, there are men who are extremely active, but whose feelings never rise above a certain level, men whom we know to be sensitive but calm.*
>
> *Third, there are men whose passions are easily inflamed, in whom excitement flares-up suddenly but soon burns out.*
>
> *Fourth, we come to those who do not react to minor matters, who will be moved only very gradually, not suddenly, but whose emotions attain great strength and durability.*
>
> *A man, whose opinions are constantly changing, even though this is in response to his own reflections, would not be called a man of character. The term is applied only to men whose views are stable and constant.*

Clausewitz refers to the man "whose opinions are constantly changing" and relates it to character. Such behavior often shows up in a manager's indecisiveness, lack of vision, unwillingness to attack a problem, or reluctance to pursue an opportunity with vigor and boldness. These displays of negative behavior in leadership are often too visible to hide from employees.

Employees can understand the need for a flexible managerial style or even a certain amount of unconventional behavior, if it is understood and accepted as part of a leader's inherent personality. However, they are unable to tolerate inconsistency and sudden erratic mannerisms, particularly if there is no apparent reason for what could be perceived as chaotic behavior. Like an epidemic, such damaging traits can spread to all those who are exposed to them.

> *Action can never be based on anything firmer than instinct, a sensing of the truth. Nowhere are differences of opinion so acute as in conflict, and fresh opinions never cease to batter at one's convictions.*
>
> *It is evident how greatly strength of character depends on balanced temperament. Most men of emotional strength and stability are therefore men of powerful character as well.*

Clausewitz's comment that "strength of character depends on balanced temperament" is another way of saying, "remain calm and firm and avoid being easily unbalanced by negative events." Often this effect can be achieved by looking at the big picture—or, more pragmatically, focusing on the long-term vision of your operation as a way of gaining an unclouded perspective.

In such a state of physical and mental composure, you are in a better state of mind to reduce any emotions of anger, fear, worry, or resentment. If left unattended, those feelings can cause you to lose your grip on the situation and possibly end up losing your advantage to a rival.

> *Appropriate talent is needed at all levels if distinguished service is to be performed. But history and posterity reserve the name of genius for those who have excelled in the highest positions, since here the demands for intellectual and moral powers are vastly greater.*

If we then ask what sort of mind is likeliest to display the qualities of business genius, experience and observation will both tell us that it is:

The inquiring, rather than the creative mind, the comprehensive rather than the specialized approach, the calm rather than the excitable head, to which in conflict we would choose to entrust the fate of our personnel and the safety and honor of our organization.

20

Strategy (Part A)

Clausewitz

Among the many factors in a conflict with a determined rival that cannot be measured, physical effort is the most important.

Unless it is wasted, its exact limit cannot be determined. But it is significant that it takes a powerful mind to drive his group to the limit.

Our reason for dealing with physical effort here is that, like danger, it is one of the great sources of friction in conflict. Because its limits are uncertain, it resembles one of those substances that makes the degree of its friction exceedingly hard to gauge.

APPLICATIONS

Physical energy expended by personnel under prolonged and stressful conditions should be a major concern to any manager. The consequences of fatigue, which is certain to impact morale, can affect the ability of both manager and subordinates to make lucid decisions. And it is likely to make the critical difference between success and failure in reaching planned objectives.

It is noteworthy, too, that Clausewitz looks at physical energy as a form of friction, which he says is difficult to measure. Nevertheless, the physical dimensions affecting performance should be carefully watched at all personnel levels.

As Sun Tzu points out in Part 1: "Pay heed to nourishing the troops; do not unnecessarily fatigue them. Unite them in spirit; conserve their strength. Make unfathomable plans."

Organizations respond in various ways to the issue of how their staffs relate to expending physical energy and the resulting impact of fatigue and friction on job performance. Their approaches consider such variables as attitudes, morale, and physical and mental well-being. They also include creature comforts, pathways to professional growth, and confident feelings about job security.

> *By intelligence we mean every sort of information about the rival, which is the basis, in short, of our own plans and operations.*
>
> *If we consider the actual basis of this information, how unreliable and transient it is, we soon realize that conflict is a flimsy structure that can easily collapse and bury us in its ruins.*
>
> *These are difficult enough to apply when plans are drafted in an office, far from the sphere of action.*
>
> *The leader must trust his judgment and give his hopes, and not his fears, the benefit of the doubt. Only thus can he preserve a proper balance.*

Notwithstanding Clausewitz's mistrust of intelligence, such an activity absolutely forms the underpinnings of strategy development. For instance:

If you are to determine the weaknesses and strengths of a competitor, then intelligence gathering is required.

If you are to develop a maneuver to skirt areas of strength and attack weaknesses, intelligence is needed to deploy your resources at a decisive point.

If you are to identify a market position in which to concentrate, intelligence is essential to the selection.

There is one hopeful conclusion to take away about the intelligence issue: Reliable market and competitor intelligence are essential for the reasons mentioned above. However, it is equally essential that vigorous efforts are made to validate, confirm, and reconfirm incoming intelligence.

Then, level-headed judgment, intuition, experience, and a positive mindset are required to apply the intelligence in developing strategies. The human factor, therefore, still remains one of the all-important variables in decision-making.

Everything in conflict is very simple, but the simplest thing is difficult. The difficulties accumulate and end by a kind of friction that is inconceivable unless one has experienced conflict.

Just as the simplest and most natural movements, walking, cannot easily be performed in water, in conflict it is difficulty for normal efforts to achieve even moderate results.

Friction is the only concept that more or less corresponds to the factors that distinguish real conflict from conflict on paper.

This tremendous friction, which cannot be reduced to a few points, is everywhere in contact with chance. It brings about effects that cannot be measured, just because they are largely due to chance.

According to Clausewitz, friction in its innumerable forms remains chronic and ever-present in market confrontations. For personnel enduring such an unsettling environment, any effort on your part to mitigate their harmful effects should be actively pursued. One remedial approach is through ongoing, practical training.

For instance, market maneuvers often require bold moves to throw competitors off track. Such maneuvers can only be carried out by individuals who exhibit the skills and discipline honed through ongoing training.

The unfaltering lesson endures: Only the skilled will survive. And the quality of your individuals is far superior to their quantity. Ultimately, it could become a key differentiator in a conflict.

Consequently, don't sacrifice quality. If you do, there is reason to expect failure—unless the competition is far inferior to you.

Sun Tzu adds this perspective (from Part 1): "A skilled commander selects his men and they exploit the situation. Now the valiant can fight, the cautious defend, and the wise counsel. Thus, there is none whose talent is wasted."

While no situation offers certain results, as Clausewitz points out with the uncertainty of friction and chance, it is axiomatic that the skilled and watchful eyes of highly trained and motivated individuals can turn disadvantage to advantage and prevent an advantage from turning into a route.

> *We have identified danger, physical exertion, intelligence, and friction as the elements that combine to form the atmosphere of conflict that impedes activity.*
>
> *Is there any lubricant that will reduce this abrasion? Only one. And a leader will not always have it readily available: real-world experience.*
>
> *To plan campaigns so that some of the elements of friction are involved, which will train individuals' judgment, common sense, and resolution, is far more worthwhile than inexperienced people might think.*
>
> *When exceptional efforts are required of him in conflict, the novice is apt to think that they result from mistakes, miscalculations, and confusion at the top. In consequence, his morale is doubly depressed. If campaigns prepare him for exertions, this will not occur.*
>
> *However, few highly experienced individuals may be in proportion to an organization. Yet their influence can be very real. Their experience, their insights, and the maturity of their character will affect their subordinates and peers.*
>
> *Even when they cannot be given authority, they should be considered as guides who can be consulted in specific eventualities.*

Clausewitz makes it quite clear about the value of "real-world experience" as well as the benefits of training—preferably through simulations that duplicate actual problems—which "will train individuals' judgment, common sense, and resolution."

21

Strategy (Part B)

Clausewitz

We have divided the acts of conflict into the two fields: tactics and strategy. The theory of tactics will unquestionably encounter the greater problems, since strategy is virtually limited to material factors.

As for strategy, dealing as it does with ends, which bear directly on the restoration of peace, the range of possibilities is unlimited.

APPLICATIONS

Clausewitz's insightful comments about "dealing ... with ends, which bear directly on the restoration of peace (and) the range of possibilities is unlimited," raise these questions:

What are the "ends," or objectives, of your business plan? Are they clearly stated and based on the strategic vision for the organization or business group over the long term?

Has enough thought been given to your organization's distinctive areas of expertise? And what will be the nature of your business as you and your team look at evolving markets and changing buying patterns?

What impact will machine learning, data analytics, and artificial intelligence have on your business? Within that context, what types of competitors will you confront? Have you consolidated your thoughts into a vision statement for your organization or business unit?*

As for the tactical short-term portion of the plan, are the objectives stated in quantitative terms for monitoring performance? As importantly, are appropriate metrics used to red-flag threats for remedial action?

This type of planning is handled by empowered individuals in what is known as *collaborative, community-based*, or *social strategy* planning. The process is taking hold in such organizations as 3M, Dutch insurer AEGON, global IT services provider HCL Technologies, Linux software provider Red Hat, and defense contractor Rite-Solutions.[†]

Clausewitz also talks about the "restoration of peace." That ideal translates to a marketplace where all competing companies share a mutual interest in actively nurturing a market for long-term profitable growth.

> *Conflict is part of man's social existence. It is a clash between major interests, which is resolved by bloodshed; and it is the only way in which it differs from other conflicts.*
>
> *Rather than comparing conflict to art, we could more accurately compare it to commerce, which is also a conflict of human interests and activities.*

"Bloodshed" needs clarification, a context, a reasonable interpretation to extract any meaning from Clausewitz's usage. For instance, one can interpret it to mean a confrontation that forces a rival to exit the market with substantial losses that stagger the organization.

Another, more extreme, meaning is conflict so conclusive that the competitor goes out of business through bankruptcy. Such an explosive event would create shock waves that cause failures among a variety of businesses within a supply chain, including fringe businesses.

Not much research is needed to compile a list of industries and individual companies in the Rust Belt that have been so affected. Other consequences follow with the resulting economic devastation to large geographic areas.

Again, think of the 2013 bankruptcy of Detroit, Michigan. Or consider the 2018 bankruptcy of the iconic Sears. Within those ruins is the

---

* See Part 3 on developing a vision statement.
[†] See Appendix on how an empowered staff can use a 100-question assessment to gain a comprehensive review of a company's competitiveness and state of readiness.

alarming toll on working-class individuals and their families who suffer psychological, financial, and social upheavals.

Any method, by which strategic plans are turned out ready-made, as if from some machine, must be totally rejected.

Conflict consists of single, great decisive actions, each of which needs to be handled individually.

A leader can best demonstrate his genius by managing a campaign exactly to suit his objectives and his resources, doing neither too much nor too little.

Strategy is the use of the engagement for the conflict. The strategist must define an aim for the entire operational side of the conflict in accordance with its purpose.

Clausewitz's references to "strategic plans ... turned out ready-made, as if from some machine, must be totally rejected" and "conflict consists ... of single, great decisive actions" have significant meanings.

Not only is there a tendency to take the easier path of repeating yesterday's strategies, there is also the misguided inclination toward relegating the writing of a strategic business plan to outsiders.

A comprehensive plan is the sum of an organization's culture, its long-term objectives, and the creative input of an increasingly empowered workforce. To consign those powerful forces to an outsider means shortchanging your organization with all its unrealized potential.

The essential point: Make the plan your team's plan and not the product of the minds of others who are physically and emotionally detached from the core culture and organizational dynamics of the group.*

No matter how superbly a leader operates, there is always a subjective element in his work. If he displays a certain style, it will in large part reflect his own personality.

---

* See Part 3 for an outline of a strategic business plan.

> *But that will not always blend with the personality of the man who copies that style. Yet it would be neither possible nor correct to eliminate subjective routine or personal style entirely from the conduct of conflict.*

As for Clausewitz's points about style and personality: There is a tendency for an individual to emulate the behavior of an individual to whom he or she reports. The result of such interaction, of course, depends on the caliber of the mentor and the quality of the advice. On the whole, however, such approaches are workable.

Yet there can be a downside where copying another's style has a negative impact. An individual can lose one's identity, which embodies the innate talents that make each person extraordinarily unique. Here, again, a balance is needed to make sure that a precise cloning doesn't take place, and that any further experience and training will enhance the distinctive qualities that already exist.

> *Once it has been determined what a campaign is meant to achieve, and what it can achieve, it is easy to chart the course.*
>
> *But great strength of character, as well as great lucidity and firmness of mind, is required to follow through steadily, to carry out the plan, and not to be thrown off course by thousands of diversions.*
>
> *Take any number of outstanding men, some noted for intellect, others for their acumen, still others for boldness or tenacity of will. Not one may possess the combination of qualities needed to make him a greater than average leader.*
>
> *In a tactical situation one can see at least half the problem with the naked eye, whereas in strategy everything must be guessed at and presumed. Conviction is therefore weaker. Consequently, most leaders, when they ought to act, are paralyzed by unnecessary doubts.*

Clausewitz's point about being "paralyzed by unnecessary doubts" has a very human and personal sound to it. His writings describe all the possible reasons for doubt, such as the innumerable areas of friction that persist and the volumes of often questionable forms of intelligence that pour in. Even with those hindrances, the plan must be written, the objectives and strategies clearly stated, and tactics set in motion.

Thus, you are left to your internal strengths, which consist of years of hard-won experience, your natural intelligence, and the inherent qualities that constitute your individuality. Ultimately, therefore, you must trust in yourself.

22

Strategy (Part C)

As a continuation of the previous two chapters, Clausewitz restates the elements of strategy that affect confrontations with rivals.

He classifies them as *morale, boldness, perseverance, superiority of numbers, surprise, cunning, concentration of forces, strategic reserves,* and *economy of force.* These elements are summarized below in Clausewitz's own words without additional commentary.

Clausewitz

Morale

An organization's efficiency gains life and spirit from enthusiasm for the cause for which it fights.

An organization that maintains its cohesion under the most adverse conditions is imbued with the true competitive spirit.

The mere fact that individuals belong to an organization does not automatically mean they are equal to their tasks. Competitive spirit, then, is one of the most important morale elements in conflict.

An organization's qualities are based on the individual who is steeped in the spirit and essence of his activity; who trains in the capacities it demands and makes them his own; who applies his intelligence to every detail; who gains ease and confidence through practice and who completely immerses his personality in the task.

Boldness

Whenever boldness encounters timidity, it is likely to be the winner, because timidity in itself implies a loss of equilibrium.

Only when boldness rebels against obedience, when it defiantly ignores an expressed order, must it be treated as a dangerous offense.

Given the same amount of intelligence, timidity will do a thousand times more damage in conflict than audacity.

While strategy is exclusively the province of leaders, boldness in the rest of the organization is as important a factor in planning as any other competitive virtue.

More can be achieved with an organization drawn from people known for their boldness, and where a daring spirit has always been nurtured, than with an organization that lacks this quality.

A distinguished leader without boldness is unthinkable. We consider this quality the first prerequisite of the great leader.

Perseverance

A leader engaged in competitive conflict is constantly bombarded by reports and data, both true and false; by errors arising from fear or negligence or hastiness; by disobedience born of right or wrong interpretations; or by accidents that nobody could have foreseen.

If a man were to give in to these pressures, he would never complete an operation. Perseverance is the essential counterweight, provided that no compelling reasons intervene to the contrary.

Moreover, there is hardly a worthwhile enterprise in conflict whose execution does not call for infinite effort, trouble, and difficulty.

As a man under pressure tends to give in to physical and intellectual weakness, only great strength of will can lead to the *objective. It is steadfastness that will earn the admiration of the world and of posterity.*

Superiority of Numbers

Superiority of numbers is only one of the factors that determine victory. Superior numbers, far from contributing everything or even a substantial part to victory, may actually be contributing very little, depending on circumstances.

Superiority varies in degree. The strategy principle is that as many resources as possible should be brought into the engagement at the decisive point.

To achieve strength at the decisive point depends on the strength of the organization and on the skill with which this strength is employed. The first rule, therefore, should be: Put the largest amount of resources possible into the engagement.

It would be seriously misunderstanding our argument to consider numerical superiority as indispensable to victory. We merely wished to stress the relative importance.

Surprise

Surprise lies at the root of all operations, though in varying degrees depending on the nature and circumstances of the operation.

The two factors that produce surprise are secrecy and speed. Both presuppose a high degree of energy on the part of the organization and the leader; they require great efficiency. Surprise will never be achieved under lax conditions and conduct.

Basically, surprise is a tactical device, because in tactics, time and space are limited in scale. In strategy, surprise becomes more feasible the closer it occurs to the tactical realm, and more difficult as it approaches the higher levels of policy.

For the side that can benefit from the psychological effects, the better it may turn out; for the rival could find himself incapable of making coherent decisions.

Cunning

Cunning is itself a form of deceit. Yet not deceit in the ordinary sense of the word, since no outright breach of faith is involved.

The use of a trick or stratagem permits the intended victim to make his own mistakes, which, combined in a single result, suddenly changes the nature of the situation before his very eyes.

If we consider strategy as the art of skillfully exploiting force for a larger purpose, then no human characteristic appears so suited to the task of directing and inspiring strategy as the gift of cunning.

We conclude that an accurate and penetrating understanding is a more essential asset for the leader than any gift for cunning. Although the latter will do no harm so long as it is not employed at the expense of more essential qualities of character.

The bleaker the situation, with everything concentrating on a single desperate attempt, the more readily cunning is joined to daring.

Concentration of Forces in Space

The best strategy is always to be very strong; first in general, and then at the decisive point. There is no higher and simpler law of strategy than that of keeping one's forces concentrated.

No force should ever be detached from the main body unless the need is definite and urgent. We hold fast to this principle and regard it as a reliable guide.

Incredible though it sounds, it is a fact that resources have been divided and separated countless times, without the leader having any clear reason for it. This folly can be avoided completely as soon as concentration of force is recognized as the norm—and every separation as an exception that must be justified.

In a strategic as well as in a tactical situation, we might be tempted to seek initial success with a minimum of personnel, in order to retain strong reserves for the final struggle. Whenever failure can be predicted with any degree of certainty, holding any part in reserve for later use would be unthinkable.

Consequently, it cannot be the intent of the strategist to make an ally of time for its own sake, by committing forces gradually. All forces intended and available for a strategic purpose should be applied simultaneously.

The Strategic Reserve

A reserve has two distinct purposes: One is to prolong and renew the action. The second is to counter unforeseen threats.

The need to hold a force in readiness for emergencies may arise in strategy. Hence there can be such a thing as a strategic reserve, but only when emergencies are conceivable.

In a tactical situation, where we frequently do not even know the rival's intentions until we see them, we must always be prepared for unforeseen developments.

It is thus an essential condition of strategic leadership that forces should be held in reserve according to the degree of strategic uncertainty.

Therefore, the view is justified that a strategic reserve becomes less essential, less useful and more dangerous to use, the more general its intended purpose.

One man thinks of a strategic reserve as the peak of wise and cautious planning. Another rejects the whole idea, including that of a tactical reserve. This kind of confused thinking actually affects reality.

Economy of Force

The man of action must at times trust in the sensitive instinct of judgment, derived from his native intelligence and developed through reflection, which almost unconsciously hits on the right course.

One of these features is always to make sure that all forces are involved—always to ensure that no part of the whole force is idle.

If a segment of one's force is located where it is not sufficiently busy with the opponent, then these forces are being managed uneconomically. In this sense they are being wasted, which is even worse than using them inappropriately.

When the time for action comes, the first requirement should be that all parts must act. Even the least appropriate task will occupy some of the rival's forces and reduce his overall strength, while completely inactive personnel are neutralized for the time being.

23

The Engagement in General

APPLICATIONS

If you accept Clausewitz's timeless truth that a major competitive campaign consists of "a number of important engagements, all confined into one whole," then a business plan provides a framework for developing more precise objectives and strategies.

Such a strategic framework could include any of the following campaigns, each intermingled with a "multitude of conditions":

- Campaigns to reclaim a former market position
- Defensive campaigns to retain a share of market in a key region
- Campaigns to neutralize a competitor's advantage by exploiting such areas as poor product and service performance, lapses in technology, problems with the supply chain, or inept leadership
- Campaigns to expand into underserved and emerging market niches
- Campaigns to enter new businesses

- Campaigns to introduce new products into existing markets and existing products into new markets
- Campaigns of opportunity initiated by upward pressures from junior-level managers where empowerment is active

What do we mean by neutralization of the rival? Simply the reduction or elimination of his forces' capabilities—either completely or enough to make him stop the confrontation.

The question whether a simple campaign or a more complex one will be the more effective is answered in favor of the simple campaign.

If the opponent decides on a simpler campaign, one that can be carried out quickly, he will gain the advantage and wreck the grand design. So, in the evaluation of a complex campaign, every risk which may be run must be weighed.

Wherever this is possible we must choose the shorter path. We will find that an active, courageous, and resolute adversary will not leave us time for long-range intricate schemes. This is proof enough of the superiority of the simple over the complex.

Decisions related to complexity vs. simplicity involve additional issues to consider. Complex plans open possibilities for mistakes, especially where coordination is needed among individuals in diverse functions and at various locations. Correct timing is also a factor where key managers have not fully internalized the intricacies of the plan.

Then there is the parallel issue of speed as a vital component in implementing strategy. Meaning: Rarely has an overlong, dragged-out, and complex campaign proved successful. Exhaustion through the excessive draining of resources damages more companies than almost any other factor.

One company, Intel, illustrates this concept. According to analysts, the company was caught off-guard by the rapid transition to and subsequent demand for new chip designs to power smartphones and tablets. The company's central focus had been on high-performance chips for big machines.

A newly installed CEO instantly recognized the urgency before an "active, courageous, and resolute adversary" dominated the field. In a strategy meeting, he issued a straight-forward, austere assignment to attending executives—to submit campaign plans directed at a single imperative objective: "Establish a dominant position in the market for mobile devices."

> *If by skillful deployment one can place the opponent at such a disadvantage that he cannot continue the campaign without risk, we can say that at this point we have beaten him.*
>
> *In deciding whether to continue the engagement, it is not enough to consider the loss of personnel and other resources, one needs to weigh the loss of morale, order, courage, confidence, cohesion, and the plan.*
>
> *In the engagement, the loss of morale has proved the major decisive factor.*
>
> *This is the time for the victor to consolidate his gains. The rival's morale will gradually recover, order will be restored, and his courage will return. In such cases only a very small portion, if any, of the hard-earned superiority will remain.*

Clausewitz makes extensive references to the power of morale. As he emphatically points out:

> *In the engagement, the loss of morale has proved the major decisive factor.*

Consider the following fundamentals for creating a morale advantage:

- Manage through availability and visibility. Show genuine interest by listening to employees' problems, complaints, and other urgent issues.
- Manage with integrity and transparency. To the extent that you can reveal sensitive information to personnel, explain future plans.

- Plan campaigns with input from others. The cross-functional team is exceptionally useful to create a collaborative environment where empowered individuals can share their expertise.
- Support an agile, spirited, and entrepreneurial workplace through ongoing training.
- Communicate often and openly about the vision, strategic objectives, and successes of the organization or business group.

> *Each engagement reaches a point when it may be regarded as decided. To reopen it would constitute a new engagement rather than the continuation of the old one.*
>
> *We may, therefore, ask what constitutes this moment of decision, this point of no return at which fresh forces will be too late to save the day:*
> *Where the purpose of the engagement is the possession of some object, the decisive moment is reached when this object is lost.*
> *Where the purpose of the engagement is the possession of a certain location, the decisive moment is usually reached when it is lost.*
> *When the successive application of force is no longer advantageous; and if the individuals involved have lost their unity and effectiveness, the decisive moment is lost.*
>
> *If a losing engagement can be turned into a success, the initial loss not only disappears, it becomes the basis for a greater victory. The magic of victory and the curse of defeat can change the elements of a campaign.*
>
> *It is better to retrieve a losing engagement before its close, rather than fight a second engagement later on.*

Clausewitz provides three criteria for determining when it is too late to save a campaign. Yet there are gray areas to consider before letting go:

First, will exiting a market niche or eliminating a product from the line provide the acceptable financial results to support withdrawal? Second, how will the move affect relationships with customers, as well as the viability of the entire product line? Third, will any open gap signal to an astute competitor an unexpected opportunity to exploit?

If an engagement were considered lost each time it took a definite turn, no additional forces would be committed in the hope of saving it.

The leader hopes that by dint of greater efforts, by whatever morale is left among the personnel, by surpassing himself, or by sheer fortune, he will be able to reverse his fortunes just once more. And he will keep at it for as long as his courage and judgment allow.

The following indicators serve as a kind of compass by which a leader can tell the direction in which his engagement is going:

1. *The psychological effect exerted by the leader's moral stamina.*
2. *The wasting away of one's own personnel at a rate faster than that of the opponent.*
3. *The amount of ground lost.*

Even these are not the real moments of decision. An answer that gradually emerges is the domineering pride of a victory.

On the other hand, there is the voice of reason counseling against spending all one has, against gambling away one's last resources, and in favor of retaining whatever is necessary for an orderly retreat.

No matter how highly rated the qualities of courage and steadfastness may be, no matter how small the chance of victory may be, the leader who goes for it with all the power at his disposal will face a point beyond which persistence becomes desperate folly. And that can never be condoned.

And should the "the domineering pride of a victory" take hold, there is a potentially dark side: complacency. Whereas winning excites the mind, improves confidence, and motivates individuals to push forward with drive, courage, and a mindset of determination, it also contains the seeds of problems.

Planning could become slipshod, emerging technologies overlooked, significant market intelligence ignored, and training neglected. Any or all of these factors can cause the past winner to become a future loser.

There is yet a flip side to that point of view to consider. If "an engagement was considered lost," the loser can learn from his/her costly mistakes and, through good leadership, rally personnel with an intense desire to win. Such an effort can often give the psychological edge to create a turnaround.

Then, there is Clausewitz's classic statement to think about: "In (conflict) the result is never final … merely a transitory evil."

24

Attack and Defense (Part A)

Clausewitz

What is the concept of defense? The parrying of a blow. What is its characteristic feature? Awaiting the blow. It is this feature that turns any action into a defensive one. It is the only test by which defense can be distinguished from attack.

A campaign, then, is defensive if we await the attack—await, specifically, the appearance of the rival. A campaign is also defensive if we wait for our area to be occupied.

In each of these cases the characteristic of waiting and deflecting is germane to the general concept of conflict.

But if we are really waging a campaign, we must return the opponent's blows. And these offensive acts in a defensive conflict come under the heading of defense. In other words, our offensive takes place within our own positions or areas of operations.

Thus, a defensive campaign can be fought in offensive encounters. And in a defensive clash, we can employ our units offensively.

So the defensive form of conflict is not a simple shield, but a shield made up of well-directed movements.

APPLICATIONS

Clausewitz talks about a "defensive campaign (that) can be fought in offensive encounters." He makes the convincing statement that there must be an attack or counter-attack component to defense. The classic case of Xerox (previously mentioned in Chapters 9 and 11) illustrates his concept.

Decades ago, when Xerox created the market for xerography, the company initially focused on large companies with its large copiers. If we introduce Clausewitz's concept of defense into this example, Xerox used passive resistance to defend its position. That is, it left exposed a vast market among small and mid-size companies for small, table-top copiers.

Astute Japanese makers of copiers, such as Canon, Sharp, and Ricoh, saw the opening and attacked that vacant market without opposition. Once secured with a solid foothold in North America, they made the next expansive move of going upscale where they confronted Xerox head-on in its big copier stronghold.

The company eventually righted itself and defended its position over the following decades and recovered a good deal of its market share. Clausewitz's prudent approach that "the defensive form of conflict is not a simple shield, but a shield made up of well-directed movements" is still valid.

What is the object of defense? Preservation. It is easier to hold ground than to take it. What follows is that defense is easier than attack, assuming both sides have equal means.

Just what is it that makes preservation and protection so much easier? It is that time, which is allowed to pass unused accumulates to the credit of the defender. He reaps where he did not sow.

Any omission of attack—whether from bad judgment, fear, or lethargy—accrues to the defender's benefit. It is a benefit rooted in the concept and object of defense; it is in the nature of all defensive action.

Another benefit, one that arises solely from the nature of conflict, derives from the advantage of position, which tends to favor the defense.

But defense has a passive purpose: preservation. And attack has a positive one: conquest. The latter increases one's own capacity to wage conflict; the former does not.

If defense is the stronger form of conflict, it has a negative object in that it should be used only so long as weakness compels. And it should be abandoned as soon as we are strong enough to pursue a positive objective.

Leaders accept defense as the stronger form, even when they personally would rather attack.

Clausewitz acknowledges that leaders "would rather attack." Yet, he presents a convincing and lucid argument for using defense, as long as there is a "parrying" or offensive component to the defense.

Let us examine the factors that lead to victory in an engagement. At this stage we are not concerned with numerical superiority, courage, training, or other qualities of an organization.

Even general superiority of numbers is not relevant, since numbers, too, are usually a given quantity in which a leader has no say. Moreover, these matters have no special bearing on attack and defense.

Only three things seem to us to produce decisive advantages: (1) Surprise, (2) the benefit of terrain, and (3) concentric attack (indirect maneuver).

Surprise becomes effective when we suddenly face the opponent at one point with far more personnel than he expected. This type of numerical superiority is quite distinct from numerical superiority in general.

Clausewitz's advice takes on greater meaning if you compare "the benefit of terrain" to the overall characteristics of the marketplace. Further, to take advantage of the "three things (that) produce decisive advantages," the defender must maintain strong customer relationships, support a firm market infrastructure to sustain growth, reinforce a reliable logistical framework, and strengthen a credible company or brand reputation.

In particular, the underpinning for those advantages should rely on ongoing intelligence about the unique characteristics and changing behaviors of the markets.

For example, Caterpillar, the giant construction and mining equipment maker, collects, stores, and dissects huge volumes of digital information, also known as *big data*. The company factory-installs into its trucks, backhoes, bulldozers, and other machinery sensors, radios, GPS receivers, and specialized software.

The move is all part of Caterpillar's global technology platform, which connects to an intelligent network that can monitor its equipment and provide beneficial reports on equipment repairs, operator usage patterns, and other valuable nuggets of information.

Disseminating those reports to equipment owners and dealers solidifies relationships along the supply chain. For Caterpillar's management, the ongoing flow of intelligence provides fresh selling opportunities for marketing and solid intelligence for service engineers to preempt and solve potential equipment problems. And meaningful data is available to product developers for new product designs and applications.

25

Attack and Defense (Part B)

Clausewitz

Part of the strategic success lies in timely preparation for a tactical victory. The main factors responsible for bringing about strategic effectiveness include the following*:

1. *The advantage of terrain*
2. *Surprise, either by actual engagement or by deploying unexpected strength, at certain points*
3. *Concentric attack (indirect maneuver)*
4. *Strengthening the area of operations*
5. *Obtaining popular support*
6. *Morale*

    As regards surprise and initiative, however, it must be noted that they are infinitely more important and effective in strategy than in tactics.

    Surprising the rival by concentrating superior strength at certain points relates to tactics. If the defender were compelled to spread his forces over several points, the attacker would reap the advantage of being able to throw his full strength against any one of them.

---

* This is a more expansive list than the one Clausewitz indicates in Chapter 24.

APPLICATIONS

Clausewitz supports his viewpoint about "surprising the rival by concentrating superior strength at certain points" with comments from previous chapters, which apply to attack and defense:

"As much resources as possible should be brought into the engagement at the decisive point. Whether these forces prove adequate or not, we will at least have done everything in our power."

"Conflicts consist of a large number of engagements, great and small, simultaneous or consecutive. Each of these has a specific purpose relating to the whole."

"Resistance is a form of action, aimed at reducing enough of the rival's power to force him to abandon his intentions."

"If a mere presence is enough to cause the opponent to abandon his position, the objective has been achieved."

"In conflict many roads lead to success. They range from wasting the rival's resources and rendering him harmless, his loss of a favorable field position, to passively awaiting the rival's attacks. Any one of these may be used to overcome the opponent's will."

We have already stated that defense is the more effective form of conflict. It is a means to win a victory that enables one to take the offensive; that is, to proceed to the objective of the conflict.

While he is enjoying this advantage, he must strike back, or he will court destruction. Prudence bids him strike while the iron is hot and use the advantage to prevent a second onslaught.

If it is not in the leader's mind from the start, if it is not an integral part of his idea of defense, he will never be persuaded of the superiority of the defensive form.

If you see value in Clausewitz's concepts about attack and defense, then consider incorporating his thinking into planning meetings with members of your staff. Similarly, think about bolstering training sessions by adding content for both strategic and tactical applications.*

Further, a case can be made for including sales personnel in similar training. That is, think of a sales representative as a general manager of a sales territory who could write a strategic plan for growth, as well as demonstrate tactical skill in mounting a competent defense against competitors.†

> *At this point let us consider how offensive campaigns can fail without a decisive battle being fought:*
>
> *The aggressor enters a defender's territory, but then begins to have doubts about risking a decisive campaign. He halts and faces his rival, acting as if he had made a conquest.*
>
> *At that point the attacker will wait for a favorable turn of events to exploit. As a rule, there is no reason to expect such a favorable turn. It is therefore a fresh delusion.*
>
> *By way of excusing his inaction, the leader will plead inadequate support and cooperation. He will talk of insurmountable obstacles, and look for motives in the most intricately complicated circumstances.*
>
> *He will fritter his strength away in doing nothing; or rather in doing too little to bring about anything but failure. Meanwhile the defender is gaining time, which is what he needs most.*
>
> *The obvious and simple truth is that failure was due to fear of the rival's forces.*

Clausewitz's references to "excusing his inaction, the leader will plead inadequate support and cooperation ... talk of insurmountable obstacles." Often, such an expression is the result of negative emotions triggered by a

---

* It is my firm opinion that personnel in mid-management positions should be able to think strategically with a long-term outlook about his or her product line or market segment. Such a role should be in addition to the immediacy of tactically confronting an aggressive competitor.
† I made this recommendation in an earlier chapter. Part 3, "Applications," provides content and a format to set a training program in motion.

range of psychological forces. One of these is an individual's deep-rooted fear of failure, which has the insidious effect of shutting down the mind and creating a type of paralysis or inability to take action.

That expression is particularly troublesome when courage is the essential ingredient in preparing for a defense, followed by offensive action. "The requisite for a man's success as a leader is that he be perfectly brave," declared the eminent strategist Baron Antoine-Henri de Jomini.

Courage is defined as the act of determination in a specific situation. It becomes a character trait only if it becomes a mental habit. As Clausewitz previously pointed out: "Intellect in itself is not courage. There are ample numbers of brilliant individuals who simply do not have what it takes to recognize that bold actions are essential elements for timely and appropriate actions."

Often, it is for the individual to arouse the inner sense of courage and push aside the awful feelings that can creep into the mind and take control of his or her actions. That is where training, discipline, and experience need to kick in to overcome negative emotions.

It is also useful to think of a confrontation as a contest of one mind against another's mind—the mind of one manager pitted against the mind of a competing manager who may be challenged by similar emotions. You want to be the one who prevails and moves forward.

26

Defense of an Area of Operations

Clausewitz

In conflict, what is meant by the opponent's organization?

If the defender's forces are neutralized; in other words, overcome and incapable of further resistance, the organization is automatically lost.

On the other hand, loss of the organization does not necessarily entail neutralization of the forces; they can exit of their own accord and reenter more easily later on.

It is always more important to neutralize forces than to hold on to territory. Possessing territory will become an end in itself only where those means are not enough.

APPLICATIONS

Clausewitz refers to "possessing territory will become an end to itself." Territories, in turn, compare with market segments where competitors routinely battle for dominance. Such is the case with the intense competition in the race to dominate the tablet market.

The magnitude of the conflict occurred when Apple, Nokia, and Microsoft each introduced new tablets on the same day. Those devices competed for consumer attention against several models released around the same period by other tech heavyweights, including Amazon and Samsung.

And in the cloud business, Amazon Web Services held a dominant position, while latecomers, such as Microsoft's Azure and Google's Cloud Platform, tried to secure and "hold on to territory."

As with virtually every active market, competitors are either in a state of attack or defense. Therefore, what criteria can help you determine how much marketing, financial, and personnel resources to concentrate on a segment?

You can use the following generally accepted guidelines to supplement your firm's benchmarks:

- Measurability. Can you quantify the segment by demographic, geographic, or behavioral factors?
- Accessibility. Do you have direct or indirect access to the market through a supply chain?
- Substantiality. Is the segment of adequate size to warrant your attention as a viable segment? What is the outlook for the segment: declining, maturing, or growing?
- Profitability. Does the segment provide sufficient profitability (or return on investment) to make the effort worthwhile? What is the timeline?
- Compatibility with the competition. To what extent do competitors have an interest in the segment? Is it of active interest or of negligible concern? What is the likelihood that any will mount an active defense?
- Effectiveness. Do your people have acceptable skills and resources to serve the segment effectively?
- Defense capability. Does your firm have the capabilities and resources to defend itself against the attack of a major competitor, and then, in keeping with Clausewitz's concepts, be able to go to on the offensive?

A major engagement is a collision between two centers of gravity. The more forces we can concentrate in our center of gravity, the more certain and massive the effect will be.

A center of gravity is always found where the mass is concentrated most densely. It presents the most effective target for a blow.

Consequently, any partial use of force not directed toward an objective that cannot be attained by the victory itself should be condemned.

The basic condition, however, does not consist merely in the greatest possible concentration of forces. They must also be deployed in a way that enables them to fight under sufficiently favorable circumstances.

Clausewitz refers to the center of gravity "where the mass is concentrated most densely." Also known as the decisive point, it is "the most effective target for a blow."

What, specifically, is a decisive point and how can you find it? There are numerous possibilities to choose from when selecting a center of gravity for a concentrated effort. The general guideline is that it represents the competitor's specific weakness or general area of vulnerability.*

The search begins by conducting a line-by-line comparative analysis that would expose your strengths against a competitor's weaknesses. The analysis includes a wide range of factors, including markets, technology, products and services, corporate culture, and the caliber of personnel.

It covers leadership and financial resources, as well as all those areas that affect the efficiency and performance of a company's ability to deal with a competitive situation. When it is completed, you will be better able to develop a defensive/offensive strategy that "enables them to fight under ... favorable circumstances."†

McDonald's, the fast-food chain, illustrates "how to hit the opponent's exact center of gravity." Recognizing that individuals between the ages of 18 and 32 represented an enormous group in which they needed to retain a strong foothold for future growth, McDonald's focused on that segment known as *millennials*.

---

* In this discussion on center of gravity against competitors, the assumption is that the decisive point also represents a viable marketplace of customers.

† See the Appendix for tools to assist you in conducting a comparative analysis.

The competitive issue, however, was that feisty adversaries such as Five Guys, Chipotle, and Subway were after that group as well, thereby threatening McDonald's defense.

While carefully monitoring competitive moves and at the same time observing the group's changing tastes, McDonald's launched its market response by focusing on new food offerings that could be made to order in 60 seconds and would satisfy its stringent fast-food requirements of time, speed, and convenience.

> *We feel that where a decisive battle is unavoidable, and where one is not quite sure of victory to begin with, in such cases a fortress capable of resistance is a powerful argument for retiring behind it to seek the decision.*
>
> *We therefore think that no defensive measure in a dangerous situation is so simple and as effective as the choice of a good position close to a substantial fortress.*

Clausewitz's meaning of "fortress" is a formidable physical structure. From a business viewpoint, a broader definition can serve a similar function. For instance, a fortress can be likened to defensible patents, long-term contracts, strong logistical networks, proprietary technologies, branding, and any other fortress-like protection that would serve as an effective "choice of a good position."

> *The natural goal of all campaign plans is the turning point at which attack becomes defense.*
>
> *If one were to go beyond that point, it would not merely be a useless effort which could not add to success. It would in fact be a damaging one, which would lead to a reaction.*
>
> *But he must know the point not to overshoot the target. Otherwise, instead of gaining new advantages, he can disgrace himself.*
>
> *This is why the great majority of leaders will prefer to stop well short of their objective rather than risk approaching it too closely.*

> *And that is why those with high courage and an enterprising spirit will often overshoot it and so fail to attain their purpose.*
>
> *Only the leader who can achieve great results with limited means has really hit the mark.*

Clausewitz refers to his often-mentioned comment that the "natural goal of plans is the turning point at which attack becomes defense."

Next, in unusually strong terms, Clausewitz states that the mere notion to "overshoot the target ... he can disgrace oneself." In equally compelling terms, he indicates that the leader's obligation is to stay close to an evolving campaign, with the paramount purpose of determining the culminating point when an attack turns into a defense.

27

Plans

Clausewitz

Plans cover every aspect of a conflict, which are woven into a single operation that must have a single, ultimate objective in which all aims are reconciled.

No one starts a conflict—or rather, no one in his senses ought to do so—without first being clear in his mind what he intends to achieve by that conflict and how he intends to conduct it. The former is its political purpose; the latter its operational objective.

This is the governing principle that will set the plan's course, prescribe the scale of means and effort, which is required and make its influence felt throughout, down to the smallest operational detail.

APPLICATIONS

Clausewitz's reference to "political purpose" is best interpreted to mean the policies of the organization. Typically, policies cover the foundation operational guidelines that control an organization. They form a tangible imprint of your company's vision, its culture, and the procedures and practices that gives your organization consistency and a distinctive personality.

While policy making may be outside your area of input, it can impact heavily on how you shape your plans. As Clausewitz says, "If conflict is part of policy, then policy will determine its character. As policy becomes more ambitious and rigorous, so will conflict."

Thus, policy influences how you

- Select strategies to grow and defend your business
- Determine the parameters by which you can innovate and compete for market advantage
- Attract new talent and assign existing personnel to new levels of authority and responsibility
- Secure your position on the supply chain, with particular attention to solidifying relationships and blocking competitive threats
- Deploy your financial and human resources to exploit market opportunities

Policy, therefore, should have a legitimate and powerful influence on your business plans. It encompasses how you cultivate the growth of your markets and control the strategy options to avoid major conflicts, especially against competitors with little interest in nurturing the long-term prosperity of the marketplace.

Conflict is an instrument of policy, with the addition of other means. We deliberately use the phrase "with the addition of other means" because we also want to make it clear that conflict in itself does not suspend political intercourse or change it into something entirely different.

It is essential that intercourse continues, irrespective of the means it employs. The main lines along which events progress are political lines that continue throughout the conflict into the subsequent peace.

"Conflict is an instrument of policy" is one of Clausewitz's most famous and often repeated statements. Other translators have expressed it as "war is an extension of policy by other means."

In a business context, the strategic plan incorporates the economic, environmental, technological, and relevant market factors that face the organization. And within that framework, the plan must take into consideration the competitive issues that relate to the inevitable conflicts with rivals.

Consequently, the mere thought of developing a strategic business plan to enter a new market and face a competitive threat without considering the political meaning of the company's strategic direction is a violation of Clausewitz's salient points regarding "conflict is a continuation of political intercourse, with ... other means."

> *Having given a detailed account of conflict, we shall now consider how it should be planned. We can identify two basic principles that underlie all strategic planning, which serve to guide all other considerations.*
>
> *The first principle is that the ultimate substance of the opponent's strength must be traced back to the fewest possible sources, and ideally to one alone.*
>
> *The attack on these sources must be compressed into the fewest possible actions—again, ideally, into one. All minor actions must be subordinated as much as possible. In short the principle is: act with the utmost concentration.*
>
> *The second principle is: act with the utmost speed. No halt or detour must be permitted without good cause.*

Clausewitz's two planning principles are generally accepted in today's business practices. Unfortunately, they are not always followed. Thus, a few comments are in order for application and reinforcement.

As for the first principle, *concentration*: This classic principle is in sharp contrast to the overly common planning approach of spreading resources in several directions, covering numerous objectives, segments, and isolated actions.

Whereas the thinking may be to play it safe and cover all contingencies, instead this approach has the potentially damaging effect of dramatically exposing weaknesses and revealing areas of vulnerability. Result: The chances of failure multiply through the excessive thinning-out of resources.

What's behind this singular, straightforward principle? In practice, it means concentrating your resources on a customer group, geographic segment, or single competitor. It means finding the decisive point so that, as Clausewitz indicates, "the attack ... must be compressed into the fewest possible actions—ideally, into one."

The hardnosed evidence from history and current business methods leads unequivocally to adopting a strategy that aims at concentrating resources where you can gain superiority in as few areas as possible.

As for the second principle, *speed*: "There is no instance of a country having benefited from prolonged warfare," declared Sun Tzu (see Part 1). In applicable terms, there are few cases of overlong, dragged-out campaigns that have been successful.

"Without exception, all of my biggest mistakes occurred because I moved too slowly," declared John Chambers, former CEO of Cisco Systems.

Thus, "no halt or detour must be permitted without good cause." Extended deliberation, procrastination, cumbersome committees, layers of bureaucracy, and indecisiveness are all detriments to success. Drawn-out efforts often divert interest, diminish enthusiasm, and damage morale.

Additionally, employees become bored and their skills lose sharpness. As damaging is that the gaps created through lack of action give competitors extra time to develop strategies that can blunt your efforts. Therefore, it is in your best interests to evaluate, maneuver, and concentrate your forces in the shortest span of time.

The proverbs "opportunities are fleeting" and "the window of opportunity is open" have an intensified truth in today's markets. Speed, then, is essential for gaining the advantage and exploiting an opportunity.

CONCLUDING COMMENTS ON ORIGINS

In the previous chapters, you may have come across familiar concepts, perhaps some that you have previously incorporated into your current management practices. Perhaps, too, you may have recognized principles and ideas that you learned through a variety of educational experiences, although expressed in different verbiage.

If so, it may be reassuring to discover their roots in another discipline and written by two of the world's foremost thinkers on strategy, Sun Tzu and Carl von Clausewitz.

Finally, the primary goal of exploring the origins of strategy is to enhance your ability to think like a strategist. With such a perspective, you can apply these time-honored concepts to developing your own unique plans and strategies as you face a turbulent competitive environment with its inevitable conflicts, confrontations, and contested campaigns.

Part 3 continues with the applications of these concepts by using the platform of a strategic business plan.

Applications

Part 3

Activating a Business Strategy: Developing a Strategic Business Plan

Sun Tzu

When developing plans compare the following elements, appraising them with the utmost care:

If you say which leader possesses moral influence and is more able,

which organization obtains the advantages of nature and the terrain,

which group is better at carrying out instructions,

which individuals are the stronger,

which has the better trained managers and staff,

which administers rewards and punishments in a more rational manner,

I will be able to forecast which side will succeed and which will fail.

Clausewitz

Two basic principles underlie all strategic planning:

First, act with the utmost concentration; second, act with the utmost speed.

OVERVIEW

The following chapters merge the origins of strategy from Parts 1 and 2 with business applications for today's digital marketplace. The process begins by incorporating the central themes from Sun Tzu's and Clausewitz's statements—leadership, planning, strategy, empowerment—into a generally accepted format of a strategic business plan that can bond your staff to a common outlook (see Figure P.3.1).

And where that collaborative effect occurs, organizational silos that tend to inhibit growth begin to break down. In turn, unity encourages sharing of ideas and solving of difficult problems. The outcome: a dynamic interplay of fresh business initiatives emerge that lead to new products and additional revenue streams.

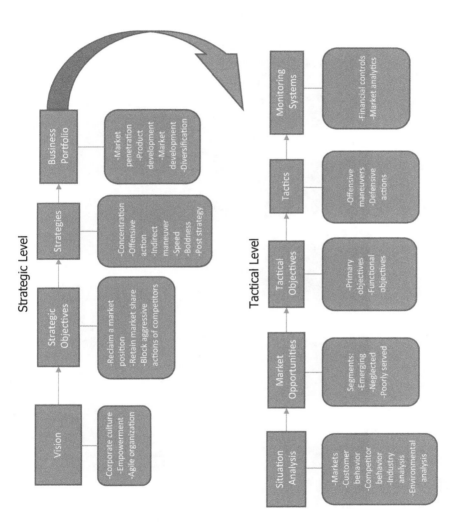

FIGURE P.3.1
Strategic Business Plan.

28

Vision

Satya Nadella CEO, Microsoft*

Part of our mission is to discover the soul of Microsoft …

(and) empower every person.

The far-reaching aim of this first section of the strategic business plan is to provide you and your team with a step-by-step process to "discover the soul" of your company or business unit. The more pragmatic purpose is to show you and your team how to write a vision statement, from which long and short-term objectives and strategies would emerge.

You begin by determining how your organization defines itself and where it will be headed in the future. You will delve into your organization's culture. Think about the state of the market and the diverse forces in which you currently operate, as well as the ones you will likely face in the future.

You will look at your organization's distinctive areas of expertise and core competencies. Examine the level of technology that will likely impact

---

* Excerpts from an interview, *Bloomberg Businessweek*, December 25, 2017 issue. Nadella's use of the word *mission* is interchangeable with the term *vision* used in this book.

your competitive position and your ability to satisfy evolving customers' needs. Completing the process will also help you and your team grasp the multiplying effect of empowerment.

Start the process by examining three components that form the underpinnings of a viable vision: *corporate culture, an empowered staff*, and *an agile organization*.

CORPORATE CULTURE

Culture encompasses the organization's values, symbols, beliefs, habits, behavior, and history. Together, they form the DNA that *is* the organization. Culture is what makes the organization a living, working entity.

It impacts the way individuals and groups interact with each other, with intermediaries, and with end-use customers. It shapes the conduct of personnel and reflects their feelings and actions.

In practice, organizational culture foretells how the company enters a market and implements its strategies, which could take the form of leader or follower, aggressiveness or timidity, speed or sluggishness. It also guides the selection of employees, influences management styles, determines the timeliness of adopting a technology, and influences the organization's structure.

An example of a spirited and robust culture is Google. The company describes its culture as "incredibly scrappy," which reflects on its leaders, employees, and overall way of conducting its business. Thus, as the nerve center of the organization, its dynamic and adaptive culture shapes how employees think and how they react under a variety of marketplace conditions.

Consequently, a positive, supportive corporate culture drives ambitious business decisions, generates customer loyalty, and ignites employee involvement in a dynamic work environment. It is the cement that binds together all the qualities and gives an organization its unique personality.

In contrast, if an organization's management shows a conscious disregard for making its culture compatible with a fast-moving digital marketplace, the company loses its competitive edge. Complacency spreads, customer focus declines, and originality dries up, all of which are extremely difficult to reverse.

EMPOWERED STAFF

In its fullest sense, empowerment considers people as unique, one-of-a-kind individuals. When used as a force multiplier, their combined energies are best suited to take advantage of technology breakthroughs that define success. In the context of today's embattled markets, that means outthinking, outmaneuvering, and outperforming competitors.

An empowered workplace is one where mistakes are tolerated with freedom from fear. Most importantly, empowerment means that executives vitally need the input of employees as much as employees need the guidance of executives. Consequently, that entails a leadership style where there is mutual respect, as well as mutual need.

Such is the case of the upscale retailer Nordstrom, where "employees are empowered to run their own business" and feel "trusted and respected," based on their long-term assessments of what is happening in their local markets.

Empowerment, then, is about shared responsibility, accountability, and achieving objectives within an organization that must adapt to change. To that end, it requires a corporate culture and corresponding workplace that aligns with the long-term strategic direction of the organization.

A reasonable interpretation of empowerment comes from Sun Tzu's writings of 2,500 years ago:

> *Individuals need no encouragement to be vigilant.*
> *Without forcing their support, the leader obtains it;*
> *without inviting their affection, he gains it;*
> *without demanding their trust, he wins it.*

AGILE ORGANIZATION

An agile organization is the third component that supports a corporate vision. A list of attributes that describe agility, based on McKinsey & Company's Organizational Health Index, is shown in Chapter 10.

These include:

quick to mobilize, nimble, collaborative, gets things done easily, responsive, allows the free flow of information, quick at decision making, empowered to act, resilient, and learns from failure.

The following merges Sun Tzu's ancient writings with McKinsey's description of agility:

> *It is according to the shapes that I lay the plans for victory, but the multitude does not comprehend this. Although everyone can see the outward aspects, none understand the way in which I have created victory.* (Power to act, learning from failure.)
>
> *Therefore, when I have won a victory, I do not repeat my tactics but respond to circumstances in an infinite variety of ways.* (Nimbleness, ease of getting things done.)
>
> *Now an organization may be likened to water. For just as flowing water avoids the heights and hastens to the lowlands, so an organization avoids strength and strikes weakness.* (Quick to mobilize, collaborative, resilient.)
>
> *And as water shapes its flow in accordance with the ground, so an organization manages its victory in accordance with the situation of the rival.* (Allowing free flow of information.)
>
> *And as water has no constant form, there are no constant conditions.* (Resilient, responsive.)

DEVELOPING A VISION STATEMENT

To involve your staff in writing a vision statement, have them answer the following six questions to "discover the soul" of your organization or business unit.

1. *What are our organization's (or group's) distinctive capabilities or areas of expertise that are unique, and which can serve as a pathway to future growth?*

These may take the form of a technology expertise, product design, or any other area contained within the marketing mix. Underlying the question is the fundamental one of understanding your customers' existing and evolving needs.

Within that framework, you and your team need to think in terms of products that could claim a competitive advantage through differentiation and new applications. That includes delving into the primary physical features and psychological influences that go into buying decisions.

The physical makeup of a product includes its design, shape, uniqueness, reliability, and overall performance. The psychological factors cover how the product or service is perceived in the consumers' minds, which determines the position it holds in the marketplace.

2. *What evolving changes are taking place among competitors that will impact our company (or product line)?*

Market dynamics create a constant state of uncertainty and instability. Often neglected in group discussions is a clear assessment of competitors' strengths and weaknesses, and whether their participation in the market is growing or declining.

The essential point is knowing where they are vulnerable in their product mix, supply chain, marketing capability, and even their leadership. Are there any gaps in market coverage that would create an opportunity for you?

Then, there is the question of which new domestic and foreign competitors are entering the market. What market niches are they filling, what comparative advantages are they using? What technologies are they featuring? And which competitive strategies and tactics appear particularly successful or unsuccessful? Are they threatening to your operations, and what are your possible counter-strategies?

3. *What segments or categories of customers will we concentrate resources on, and which can we defend against the attack of aggressive competitors?*

This question is multifaceted and includes a review of existing expertise, available resources, and the culture of your organization.

The central issues: How do the segments you plan to serve fit your company's overall vision? That also means locating the competitive position you want to hold in the marketplace, the products and services you want to market, and the customer needs you want to fulfill.

Then, there are other pragmatic considerations, such as how large the segment is and what its growth potential is. Are there enough company resources readily available to enter the market against entrenched competitors? What is the state of existing production capabilities and technologies to achieve your objectives in the evolving digitized markets?

4. *What additional functions or services are we likely to perform for customers as we see the market evolve?*

Functions relate to how well products or services satisfy, and, more specifically, how well they compare with competitors' offerings. You should assume that competitors are asking similar questions in an attempt to beat your offerings. This is where comparative analysis of key buying factors is needed to provide a more comprehensive view and a more accurate answer to the question (see Table 28.1. Comparative Analysis of Key Factors).

5. *What new technologies will we require through internal growth, acquisition, or alliances to satisfy future customer needs, which can meet and exceed those used by competitors?*

Here is where you and your team must look to the thrust of evolving technologies in such areas as artificial intelligence, deep learning, 3-D printing, robotics, and digitization.

A parallel consideration is your supply chain. How influential are middlemen in the buying process? How alert are they in keeping up with evolving technologies? A major part of an evaluation relates to their overall performance, which includes finding out how proficient they are in the use of e-commerce and social media.

6. *What business(es) should we be in over the next 5 years considering where our industry is headed, with ongoing emphasis on the evolving state of digital technologies and the elaborate promises of artificial intelligence?*

This question is another of the soul-searching ones that need reflective and insightful thinking from individuals inside and outside your firm.

You and your team's answers to the above six questions would be compressed into a statement that represents a realistic vision for your company, business unit, or product line. Then, two summary questions:

TABLE 28.1

Comparative Analysis of Key Factors

Product/Service	Price	Marketing	Supply Chain	Leadership/Management
Quality	Discounts	Advertising: print, broadcast, TV, mobile	Channels: e-commerce	Caliber of leadership
Features	Allowances	Social media	Direct marketing	Level of employee morale
Options	Payment period	Cross-platform publishing	Distributors/ dealers	Quality of training
Applications	Credit terms	Publicity	Retail	Managerial competence related to mobilizing resources and decision-making ability
Style	Special financing	Personal selling:	Market coverage:	Level of expertise in planning and developing competitive (indirect) strategy
Brand, image, reputation		Sales force deployment	Warehouse locations and proximity to customers	Quality of data analytics and competitor intelligence
Packaging		Incentives	Inventory control and ordering systems	Organizational design related to agility, internal communications, and flow of information
Sizes		Sales aids	Physical transport and timeliness of delivery	Corporate culture related to aggressive or passive behavior toward competitors
Support services		Samples		
Warranties		Training		
Returns		Sales promotion:		
Versatility		Webinars		
Uniqueness		Trade shows		
Utility		Events		
Reliability		Demonstrations		
Durability		Sampling		
Patent protection		Contests		
Guarantees		Premiums		
		Coupons		
		Manuals		
		Telemarketing		
		Internet		

First, can your company's culture support your vision? Second, are there sufficient financial, material, and personnel resources to make that vision a reality?

Vision Statement

The following statement is an actual example of a well-written vision for a division of a company that produces medical devices. Note how it drives an expansive vision for growth in a changing marketplace:

> "Our vision is to meet the needs of consumers and healthcare providers for drug-delivery devices by offering a full line of hypodermic products and product systems. Our leadership position will be maintained through internal research and development, licensing of technology, and/or acquisitions to provide alternative administration and monitoring systems."

The company's previous statement: "Our position is to be a leader in the manufacture of hypodermic needles." That statement indicated a narrower and highly restrictive vision, which left it vulnerable to low-cost producers and with little room for opportunistic thinking and growth.

In another example, at the onset of its journey that led to phenomenal success, Airbnb began asking its own soul-searching questions to form a vision. "Why does Airbnb exist? What is its purpose? What is its role in the world?" The answer was brief, insightful, and meaningful in setting the company's direction: *Belong anywhere.*

For Airbnb's executives, these two words succinctly addressed a deep psychological need for travelers to feel part of something; that is, to experience an attachment to the lives of other people and not be alone. There was the sense of somehow being cared for by the invisible presence of those who owned the dwelling.

From Airbnb's point of view, that vision tapped into one of the fundamental needs of individuals. And the company was there to provide an alternative to the perceived impersonal experience encountered in other forms of lodging. Then, there were the practical and tangible benefits of costs, convenience, and other advantages.

Team Activity

To involve your team in writing a vision statement, have them begin by using the above six guideline questions. If your team numbers ten or more, divide them into work groups of four or five. When completed, reconvene the entire group and have each team make a presentation. Then, review all the presentations in an open meeting. The intent is to tap into the deep well of creativity that exists within each individual.

The following section, "Strategic Objectives," translates your vision into tangible outcomes.

29

Strategic Objectives

> **Sun Tzu**
>
> *Know the enemy and know yourself, in a hundred battles you will never be in peril.*
>
> *When you are ignorant of the enemy but know yourself, your chances of winning or losing are equal.*
>
> *If ignorant of both your enemy and yourself, you are certain in every battle to be in peril.*

Sun Tzu's advice about "knowing yourself" and "knowing your enemy" has a pungent truth to it when you consider the possibility of being caught off-guard by competitors that threaten your core market position or try to force you out of your traditional markets, as was done to the once venerable Kodak.*

---

* See Chapter 10 for details about the conditions that led to Kodak's situation.

If faced with such circumstances, you are left with choices: You can retreat from some market segments and downsize, as General Electric did beginning in 2018; or you can mount a costly marketing campaign to reclaim your former market position.

Whatever the choice, you are still left with the elusive issues that embody "knowing"; that is, finding the reasons why you were pushed out of a market or why you had to deviate sharply from your original business plan.

Notwithstanding that the causes may have been obvious, such as product failure, inability to deliver on time, or service problems, you still have to face the stark reality that some deep-rooted, pervasive conditions pre-existed in the organization that resulted in having to scramble for a quick turnaround.

If you and your staff are to face the challenges of recovery, then begin by joining them in answering the following questions:

Were the competitive actions that resulted in losing market share wholly unexpected? That is, was it a surprise, or could it have been avoided if accurate market intelligence were available?

Did a communications system exist within the organization that would have permitted the free flow of data from the field to the right decision-making managers who could have reacted rapidly to the danger? Better yet, was anyone at the local level empowered to react to an impending problem?

Did contingency plans exist that could have averted the crisis, thereby avoiding risky knee-jerk reactions?

Was the staff sufficiently involved, and trained, to internalize the seriousness of the situation and recommend strategies to defend the market position—including salespeople?*

To what extent, if at all, did leaders maintain a unified effort during the decline?

Why involve your staff in these questions?

First, the queries emphasize that widespread vulnerabilities could have been festering for long periods, resulting in the defending company losing

---

* The assumption is that the sales staff is, or should be, viewed as general managers of their respective sales territories. Consequently, they should be responsible and accountable for recognizing an impending competitive crisis and be able to recommend responsive strategies. Several insightful organizations have taken the lead in orienting and training their sales staffs by elevating their thinking to a strategic level.

its market position. Yet, the process could surface valuable clues about taking corrective action.*

Second, the review could stimulate ideas for developing objectives and strategies to reclaim a market position, or, more drastically, taking the business in an entirely new direction, as eventually was the case with Kodak.

Third, concurrent with the previous point, an objective would be to challenge a competitor's advantage by neutralizing its capabilities to do future harm.

Fourth, examining the sources of problems reinforces the idea that objectives should align with the vision contained in the business plan.

Table 29.1 illustrates how the medical devices company described in Chapter 28 linked its vision with strategic objectives.

TABLE 29.1

Medical Devices Company: Aligning Vision with Objectives

Vision:

Our vision is to meet the needs of consumers and healthcare providers for drug-delivery devices by offering a full line of hypodermic products and product systems. Our leadership position will be maintained through internal research and development, licensing of technology, and/or acquisitions to provide alternative administration and monitoring systems.

Objectives†:

1. Maintain our low-cost producer status while introducing new improvements to existing products.
2. Aggressively support our dominant market-share position in all market segments.
3. Retain enough manufacturing capacity to absorb our competitors' market share in existing segments, as well as serve new and emerging segments.
4. Launch new products to strengthen our leadership position in hypodermic drug delivery devices.
5. Uphold a level of 78% retail distribution and 53% retail market share for hypodermic products and product systems.
6. Increase trade distribution and block entry of competitors into the home-care segment of the market.

---

* Correcting some deep-rooted problems may be beyond your level of authority. In that instance, you would have to adjust your objectives to fit the circumstances. Otherwise you could face the same dilemma you are trying to correct.

† The company's quantitative objectives, such as sales, return-on-investment, and other metrics are not shown here. Also, the following chapter illustrates the strategies associated with these objectives

DEVELOPING STRATEGIC OBJECTIVES

The problems related to reclaiming a market position, retaining market share, or blocking aggressive actions of competitors have hit companies in virtually every industry. Such attacks have come not only from traditional competitors, but also from organizations that entered businesses from totally different fields.

One industry that has received worldwide attention is the car-sharing business. Consider Uber, Lyft, and Didi, which used disruptive technologies to upend old-line taxi companies. After losing customers, watching revenues nosedive, and even watching their drivers move to the startups, some taxi companies began fighting back to reclaim what they had lost.

They responded by outfitting their vehicles with electronic features like those used by their new adversaries. For taxi companies under the control of local governments, similar changes were mandated to retain their taxi licenses.

Thus, objectives are developed within a dynamic framework of competitors' aggressive actions, technology advancements, and changing customer behavior. They are also formed where organizational shortcomings result from an inability to mount an adequate defense of its market position.

Given those varied market conditions, what sources can you and your team use to develop objectives? The following list (a digest version of Table 28.1) consists of five categories: product/service, price, marketing, supply chain, and leadership/management.

Product/Service

This category includes such areas as quality, features, applications, packaging, technical support, and warranties. Where any are selected as objectives, determine by comparative analysis with competitive offerings if any can be used as a credible advantage.

Other possibilities exist for differentiation, such as the reformulation and redesign of a product into a line extension to reach new market niches, or to defend an existing market segment.

As for service, objectives could relate to a broad range of options, from providing customers with access to key personnel in your firm, or providing 24/7 on-site technical assistance.

Pricing

This category includes several possibilities. Referring again to the medical company in Table 29.1, one of its objectives is to maintain its status as a low-cost producer. In that instance, their managers could maneuver with numerous pricing objectives, such as discounts, allowances, payment periods, credit terms, and special financing arrangements for customers.

Marketing

Marketing presents many possibilities, including advertising, social media, personal selling, sales promotion, Internet, publicity, and telemarketing. As with the other categories, objectives should align with the corporate or business unit vision.

In the case of the medical company, marketing would support some of its objectives, such as

- Aggressively supporting its dominant market-share position in all market segments
- Launching new products to strengthen its leadership position in hypodermic drug delivery devices
- Upholding a level of 78% retail distribution and 53% retail market share for hypodermic products and product systems

Supply Chain

Here is where you look at direct and indirect channels, with an emphasis on e-commerce. If using intermediaries, your objectives could deal with increasing geographic coverage and solidifying relationships with distributors and others in the chain.

Then there are physical distribution and logistical factors, from order-entry to the physical movement of a product through the supply chain and eventual delivery to the end user. That includes exploring the use of autonomous vehicles and drones.

The medical company illustrates its supply-chain objective as *increase trade distribution and block entry of competitors into the home-care segment of the market.*

Leadership/Management

This all-encompassing category cycles back to Sun Tzu's opening statement that begins "Know the enemy (competitor) and know yourself, in a hundred battles (market campaigns) you will never be in peril."

That means gathering as much intelligence as you can about the rival's overall capabilities, including its financial condition and its ability to sustain prolonged marketing campaigns. In particular, information should relate to the caliber of leadership, the level of employee morale, the quality of training, and how it reacts to a variety of marketplace conditions.

Team Activity

In a group meeting, ask your team to set objectives to either reclaim a former market position that you may have lost, or to defend a market against aggressive competitors.

What you are looking for is for them to follow a process. For instance, using the questions listed in this chapter, they would determine what might have been the underlying causes leading to those objectives. The team should also indicate corrective actions, even if the remedies go beyond their levels of responsibility. As a follow-on, you may wish to have them develop objectives that tie in to your corporate or business vision.

The next chapter discusses strategies. These are the actions taken to achieve the objectives.

30

Strategies

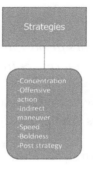

Continuing with the strategic business plan as a platform for determining where you are and where you want to go, you saw that a vision statement is the first step in imagining the future of your company or business unit. You then looked at a process for developing objectives that describe, in quantitative and non-quantitative outcomes, what you want to achieve.

Thus far, these statements indicate good intentions. Now, an action component, *strategy*, is needed to make those aims come alive. The following consists of the elements of strategy, most of which were mentioned in the Origins sections of this book: *concentration, offensive action, indirect maneuver, speed, boldness, and post-strategy.*

CONCENTRATION

Clausewitz

There is no higher and simpler law of strategy than that of keeping one's forces concentrated ... to be very strong: first in general, and then at the decisive point.

Sun Tzu

If I can determine the rival's dispositions while at the same time, I conceal my own, then I can concentrate, and he must divide.

And If I concentrate while he divides, I can use my entire strength to attack a fraction of his. There, I will be numerically superior.

Then, if I can use many to strike few at the selected point, those I deal with will be in dire straits.

Even with a 2,500-year gap in time, history, and culture, Clausewitz's and Sun Tzu's statements about concentration are remarkably similar.

The concept of concentration has been used numerous times in previous chapters to highlight that element of strategy. In applied usage, it translates to targeting your organization's resources at a single individual, organization, customer group, or market segment, defined by geographic, demographic, or behavioral criteria.

It also means concentrating on a competitor's area of vulnerability for the purpose of neutralizing its ability to upend your plans.

Additionally, concentration results in more accurate resource allocation by preventing excessive waste of human, material, and financial resources. And with the use of data analytics to pinpoint decisive points in which to concentrate, "there, I will be numerically superior" against a formidable competitor.

IBM used a concentration strategy as it sold off many of its traditional product lines in the mid-1990s, as did Apple during that same period. Walmart, one of the world's largest organizations by revenues, is among the least diversified S&P 500 companies. These efforts collectively support a strategy of concentration.

In sharp contrast is the overly common planning method of spreading resources in several directions, covering numerous objectives, segments, and isolated actions. Whereas the thinking may be to play it safe and cover all contingencies, instead this approach has the potentially damaging effect of dramatically exposing weaknesses and making a company vulnerable to competitors. Result: The chances of failure multiply through the excessive thinning out of resources.

The starting point for locating a decisive point on which to concentrate is a comparative analysis that highlights market segments where you have a clear-cut superiority. Additionally, it means being able to neutralize a competitor's attempt to upend your plans. When the analysis is completed, you are better able to develop a strategy that singles out a market in which to concentrate your resources.

The hardnosed evidence, from ancient history to current business practice, leads unequivocally to the conclusion that "keeping one's forces concentrated" gains competitive superiority.

OFFENSIVE ACTION

Sun Tzu

If courageous, a commander gains victory by seizing opportunity without hesitation.

"Seizing opportunity" requires going on the offensive. That means taking into consideration the following guidelines.

First, where a market is actively defended by an entrenched competitor, an immediate objective would be to locate a niche in which you could gain a viable position. That means focusing greater resources to make up for the initial advantages held by the defender, such as superior knowledge of the market and possibly a secure hold on key parts of the supply chain.

Second, should your offensive action lack material superiority, look to high staff morale to offset the imbalance. Conversely, if the defender's morale is weak, the bolder your actions, the greater your chances of winning. The following quote offers an insightful appraisal about morale:

Field Marshal Sir Archibald Wavell

The final deciding factor of all engagements ... is the morale of the opposing forces. Better weapons, better food, and superiority in numbers will influence morale, but it is a sheer determination to win, by whomever or whatever inspired, that counts in the end. Study men and their morale always.

Third, a high-priority, follow-up plan should be in your hand and ready to exploit the initial success. Gaining entry is only the first step, and it is likely to be an untenable one. That means you need extra resources to solidify your position, as you prepare for the inevitable response from one or more competitors.

Fourth, once you achieve the desired objectives, such as securing a solid entry into a market segment, then further offensive action ends and reverts to defending your hard-won success. However, should the plan call for further expansion, then going on the offensive, followed by the defensive cycle, would resume.

INDIRECT MANEUVER

Sun Tzu

There are not more than two methods of attack: the direct and the indirect.

Yet these two in combination give rise to an endless series of maneuvers. The direct method may be used for joining battle, but indirect methods will be needed to secure victory.

The fundamental principle underlying indirect maneuver is the avoidance of costly and often lengthy direct confrontations with a competitor. Rather, the prudent strategy is to circumvent your rival's strong points of resistance, thereby preventing unnecessary damage to your company.

An indirect approach operates in three dimensions.

First, the strategy is anchored to a line of action whereby you apply your strength against a competitor's weakness. The essence of the move is to maneuver so that your rival lacks the capability to challenge your efforts. Again, this calls for a comparative analysis that is anchored to ongoing competitor intelligence.

Second, concurrent with activating indirect moves against a competitor, your attention would be directed to serving customers' needs or resolving their problems in a manner that measurably outperforms your competitors.

Third, your aim is to achieve a psychological advantage by creating an unbalancing effect in the mind of the rival manager. That is, by means of distractions and false moves, you make it appear that you are launching your effort directly at the competitor's strengths, whereas your true purpose is to target his or her vulnerabilities.

Consequently, indirect maneuvers consist of interlocking physical and psychological forces that require strategic thinking, the ability to destabilize the competitor, and the creativity to identify areas of differentiation. Once again, the object is to circumvent direct confrontation, since competitive fighting is not the object of maneuver. Its purpose is to achieve a business objective, such as occupying a profitable and sustainable long-term position in a market. The following ancient statement provides a broad perspective on the indirect maneuver:

Sun Tzu

For to win one hundred victories in one hundred battles is not the acme of skill. To subdue the rival without fighting is the acme of skill. Supreme excellence consists in breaking the enemy's resistance without fighting.

SPEED

> **Sun Tzu**
>
> *Speed is the essence of conflict. Take advantage of the rival's unpreparedness; travel by unexpected routes and strike him where he has taken no precautions.*

Sun Tzu's statement is a steadfast truism that applies to virtually all companies and individuals.

For companies: There are few cases of overlong, dragged-out business campaigns that have been successful. Exhaustion—the excessive draining of resources—damages more companies than almost any other factor. Then, there is the problem of a cumbersome organizational framework that slows timely decisions to a crawl and wears away at prime opportunities.

Consequently, the agile organization is the ideal framework to utilize speed and maintain a capability for flexible response. "Without exception, all of my biggest mistakes occurred because I moved too slowly," declared John Chambers, former CEO of Cisco Systems.

For individuals: Drawn-out efforts divert interest, diminish enthusiasm, and depress morale. Individuals become bored and their skills lose sharpness. The gaps of time created through lack of positive results give competitors a greater chance to react and reap the benefits.

To give pragmatic reality to the element of speed, look at its strategic value through the following five propositions:

1. *Timing affects market share, product position, and customer relationships—all of which are difficult to recover once lost to a competitor.*

   Recovering a competitive position and customer loyalty are often costlier, more time consuming, and riskier than moving swiftly at the initial signs of threat. The damage is less severe and the odds better for revival.

2. *Where a company stalls and loses momentum, it signals a vigilant competitor to move in and fill a void.*

There are always alert competitors probing for weaknesses in a rival company or searching for a poorly served market segment they can exploit.

3. *Speed is a factor in preventing a product from becoming a commodity and possibly causing irreparable damage to a company's reputation.*

   Product life cycles remain a compelling reality and should be factored into the business plan. The appropriate time to develop product and market strategies to forestall maturity and decline is during the growth stage of the cycle.

4. *The risk of losing a viable position on the supply chain occurs by not moving quickly to secure key middlemen or end-use customers.*

   Timely and efficient distribution is the bedrock requirement of a successful marketing effort. Losing the position within a well-organized supply chain creates a break that is sure to be filled by a rival firm.*

5. *Speed adds vitality to a company's operations and behaves as a catalyst for growth. It impacts virtually every part of the organization and is a major factor in competitiveness.*

   Momentum elevates employee morale and tends to energize an entire organization, which adds favorably to its competitiveness. (Look again at Wavell's comments about the value of morale.)

BOLDNESS

Clausewitz

A distinguished leader without boldness is unthinkable. Therefore, we consider this quality the first prerequisite of the great leader.

---

* This factor loses some of its importance with organizations that rely on direct distribution from producer to end-user. Then speed of delivery is the key issue.

Sun Tzu

If a leader is not courageous, he will be unable to conquer doubts or create great plans.

History teaches that an enterprise accented with purpose, courage, and an affinity for boldness leads, more often than not, to successful performance. Other factors being somewhat equal, where boldness meets caution, boldness wins; it is "the first prerequisite of the great leader."

Thus, audacity in plans and action have a powerful emotional impact on the minds and subsequent behaviors of the staff, especially where they are empowered, whereas excessive caution is handicapped by a loss of stability, initiative, and momentum.

For individuals who don't have the innate personality and temperament to act with boldness, even a small measure of courage still remains a practical, and even prudent, course of action—provided, that is, that the display of daring is supported by a sound business plan, ongoing competitive intelligence, clearly stated objectives, and skillfully crafted strategies. Then your boldness is justified, with the likelihood that you will end up with profitable outcomes.

The traits that embody boldness among highly successful leaders are superior intellect, insight, and the compelling need to make things happen. The stronger the combination of these traits, the greater is their reach for changing possibilities into opportunities and then into action.

These individuals include the likes of Bill Gates, Jeffrey Bezos, Stephen Jobs, Larry Page, Sergey Brin, and Mark Spielberg. They are the ones who break through the heavy barriers that envelop mediocrity.

Boldness, then, is a force bound by a leader's personality and self-control. If disciplined, the leader can make decisions to commit resources based on the objectives of the plan and not dissipate them into inconclusive activities, such as running after some unsubstantiated lure of a Monday-morning headline that in itself is short-lived.

There are still other dimensions that relate to boldness. An organization may be infused with that strategy element for three reasons.

First, a company may deliberately recruit aggressive individuals who exhibit boldness. For instance, one organization in the electronics field sought out individuals who had active military service and graduated from a military academy. Beyond those initial credentials, only those who served as air force and navy fighter pilots, combat-experienced soldiers and marines, and submariners were hired.

Second, a company may seek bold leaders within its ranks. They would be the ones who voluntarily take on the responsibility of influencing other personnel. In so doing, they counteract the insipid tendencies that lead to complacency and lethargy. Google, for instance, builds teams known as "smart creatives" who are characterized as impatient, outspoken risk-takers.

Third, senior-level management aligns its corporate culture to foster boldness. Such a workplace tends to drive bold decisions and inspire individuals to act with a corresponding mindset. That type of culture is again illustrated by Google, where fast decision-making and flat organizational models are a corporate way of life.

POST STRATEGY

Clausewitz

The natural goal of all campaign plans is the turning point at which the attack becomes defense. If one were to go beyond that point, it would not only be useless effort, which could not add to success, it would in fact be a damaging one.

Sun Tzu

Although everyone can see the outward aspects, none understands the way in which I have created victory. Therefore, when I have won a victory, I do not repeat my tactics, but respond to circumstances in an infinite variety of ways.

The purpose of a post-strategy is to set in motion contingency plans to "respond to circumstances in a variety of ways." Without a post-strategy, your overall business plan is incomplete and can lead to shoot-from-the-hip actions. Further, it places you at the mercy of market and competitive forces with no orderly strategy to extricate yourself from the market.

Warning signals from the marketplace include such issues as competitors attacking with claims of technology breakthroughs, or sudden announcements of superior product quality. It is also defined where there are trends in declining sales, profits, market share, and customer retentions. These, then, are "the turning point at which the attack becomes defense."

A post-strategy exists on two levels.

First, you can opt to stay and defend the market for the long haul. That choice entails enhancing customer relationships, prolonging the life cycle of an existing product, replacing failing products with new or improved offerings, and managing other areas of the business, for example, service, communications, supply chain activities, and the like.

Second, should aggressive competitors make it untenable for you to remain in the market, you can exit the market after fulfilling required obligations to workers, customers, and communities. Or you may choose to reduce your presence in a market by removing products using a deliberate phasing-out process.

SUMMARY

The six elements of strategy require astute leadership, a positive corporate culture, an agile organization, an empowered staff, and reliable business intelligence, all of which is enveloped in a strategic business plan.

Finally, continuing with the medical company example from Chapter 29, three of the original six objectives are listed here to show the linkage of objectives to strategies.

Objective 1

Maintain our low-cost producer status while introducing new improvements to existing products.

Strategies

- Reduce costs by 32.5% before 2023. Maintaining low-cost producer status gives our company the widest strategic flexibility in dealing with competitive assaults on our franchise. Potential areas for cost reduction:

Overhead reductions, 4.5%
Waste reductions, 7.0%
High speed needle line, 6.5%
Sales territory redesign, 8.0%
Quality improvement and reduction in repair service, 4.0%
Packaging improvement, 2.5%
Total: 32.5

- Improve existing product through improved dosage control and improved packaging to maintain a competitive advantage.

Objective 2

Aggressively maintain our dominant market share position in all market segments.

Strategies

- Develop the Supra-Fine 111 needle to maintain superior product quality and performance versus competition, as it relates to injection comfort.
- Increase spending levels on consumer/trade support programs to provide added value to product offerings, thereby decreasing attractiveness of lower-priced alternatives while maintaining brand loyalty.
- Maintain broadest retail distribution and highest service levels to gain retailer support in promoting our brands and carrying adequate inventory levels.
- Continue health-care educational programs to gain professional recommendations at time of diagnosis and thereby maintain brand loyalty among users.

Objective 3

Launch new products to strengthen our leadership position in drug delivery devices.

Strategies

- Introduce a 40-unit syringe to address the needs of users on multiple dose therapy. Converting users to a 40-unit syringe will insulate this group against competitive initiatives.
- Develop and introduce a disposable pen-cartridge injection system to further segment the market and thereby block competitors' points of entry.
- Become a full-line supplier of drug delivery devices by broadening product offerings through internal research and development, joint venture, licensing, and acquisitions.

Embedded in these objectives and strategies are broader aims, such as protecting and defending legacy markets, as well as expanding into new user segments. Also, the company's objectives and strategies cover a wide range of activities and incorporate a variety of functions within the organization.

Thus, empowering as many people as possible from different functions, experiences, and points of view gains momentum through the participation of manufacturing, product development, finance, sales, and distribution to make the vision come alive.

The next chapter deals with the *Business Portfolio* section of the strategic business plan (Figure P.3.1.)

31

Business Portfolio

Clausewitz

In conflict even the ultimate outcome is never to be regarded as final. The outcome is merely a transitory evil, for which a remedy may still be found in a variety of possible conditions at some later date.

The purpose of this section of the plan is to show that should you face a negative competitive confrontation, the "outcome is never to be regarded as final." There is "a remedy ... in a variety of possible conditions." Although solutions could come from a variety of areas in the marketing mix, most often it relies on products and markets.

Thus, the product portfolio offers an organized way to find strategies within existing products and markets, as well as in new products and markets.

As a starting point, refer again to your vision statement. As an overall guideline, the broader the dimension of the vision, the more expansive the range of products and markets in the portfolio. Conversely, the narrower the dimension of the vision, the more limited the content of products and markets.

The following working model illustrates how to develop a business portfolio that takes into account market penetration, product development, market development, and diversification.

- *Market penetration: Existing products to existing markets*

  List your current products to existing customer groups. Based on sales, profits, market share data, competitive position, and other pertinent information, determine if the level of market penetration meets your corporate criteria, and if possibilities exist for further growth.

  For example, think about making minor product or service changes where new data indicate changing buying patterns. Consider, too, improving product quality, instituting rapid delivery systems, increasing technical support, improving customer service, and installing digitized inventory control systems. Any one of these could enhance your market position, as well as make it more defensible against rivals.

- *Product development: New products to existing markets*

  Next, think about new products to existing markets. Ideally working with a team, consider a broader definition of the vision as a way of imagining new products.* Again, the wider the interpretation of your vision, the wider the possibilities for adding content to the portfolio.

  If too narrow, the possibility for new product ideas may be unnecessarily limiting. You may have to go back to the vision statement and modify it. Doing so opens the possibilities for innovative new products.

- *Market development: Existing products to new markets*

  Now turn in another direction for "a remedy" by taking current products into new markets. With team input, explore possibilities for market development by identifying emerging or poorly served segments in which existing products could be sold.

---

* A new product is often viewed as something new to the world. However, from a marketing viewpoint, a more pragmatic approach is to consider a product new if it is *perceived* as new by prospects and customers.

Keep in mind, too, that any risk you take is not necessarily with the products. The products already exist. The risk is in redeploying valuable resources away from your primary markets. That could mean diverting key staff from your core products. Then, there is the added investment required to enter new markets. Thus, how far afield should you go from your basic markets?

One answer is to return to your vision and use it as a guiding beacon to direct your thinking. Better yet, go back to the fundamental questions you used to develop your vision statement, such as: What business should our firm be in over the next 3–5 years? What customer segments will we serve? What additional functions are we likely to fulfill for customers? What changes are taking place in markets and the environment? How will our organization participate in that future?

- *Diversification: New products to new markets*

  This portion of the business portfolio is visionary. It involves developing new products that in some cases result from changes in buying behavior and, in turn, would open new markets. Also, new technologies evolving from artificial intelligence, deep learning, and robotics continue to create fresh opportunities for new products and services. Thus, actively thinking about this portion of the portfolio will prevent riding existing businesses into maturity and then to decline, as was illustrated in previous chapters with Kodak.

Visionary organizations such as Google, Apple, Toyota, Microsoft, and IBM, as well as numerous smaller businesses, devote time and energy to filling this portion of the portfolio. And where some organizations don't have the financial resources, they find "a variety of possible conditions" through joint ventures and other approaches.

Once again, interpret the vision in its broadest context. That is the reason for using a strategic business plan as an organized framework to come up with more accurate strategies, so that "the (negative) outcome is merely a transitory evil."

Table 30.1 graphically shows an abbreviated version of the medical company's actual business portfolio of products and markets—both existing and new.

The business portfolio completes the strategic level (top row of boxes) of the strategic business plan. The lower row of boxes in Figure P.3.1 is the tactical plan. Although it is not detailed here, it should not be considered

TABLE 30.1

Product Portfolio*

Market Penetration: Existing Products/ Existing Markets	*Product Development: New Products/ Existing Markets*
24-gauge hypodermic needle for • Diabetes • Allergies • Hospitals • Clinics • Homecare	• 32-gauge hypodermic needle • SupraFine 111 needles • 40-gauge syringe/multiple-dose therapy systems
Market Development: Existing Products/ New Markets • *Urban markets* • *Ethnic populations* • *Demographic segments* • *Pacific-rim countries*	*Diversification: New Products/New Markets* • Disposable pen—cartridge injection system • Implanted injection pumps with sensors

a stand-alone plan. It is part of the total strategic business plan consisting of both the strategic and tactical levels.

What follows in Part 4 are the origins and applications of the digital-age organization.

---

* The listings in this table are a partial representation of products and markets from the division's actual plan. Supporting information on sales, units, profits, market share, and other metrics would be included in a separate document. For a few of the new products, detailed graphics and specifications were also attached.

Further, the division's actual portfolio listed additional diseases for which hypodermic systems were needed. These, too, would be placed in the appropriate section of the portfolio. The information on population, ethnic, geographic, and demographic factors also breaks down into subsegments for review. In turn, this data drives new packaging, methods of treatment, educational programs, and types of distribution.

Part 4

Origins and Applications of the Digital-Age Organization

Sun Tzu

Now, the supreme requirements of leadership are a clear perception, the harmony of his host, a profound strategy coupled with far-reaching plans, an understanding of the seasons, and an ability to examine the human factors.

32

Evolution of the Modern Organization

Academics, consultants, and executives offer various approaches to organizational design for the digital age. Their solutions are somewhat different depending on each individual's point of view. Yet commonalities do exist in many areas.

For instance, most agree that today's organizational structure should incorporate openness, agility, and flexibility. Yet, within such a structure, a prevailing force is often felt but not seen. It permeates the work environment with feelings of changeability, urgency, and uncertainty.

In that unsettling state, individuals are called on to accomplish outstanding feats through innovation and inventiveness. Former Cisco CEO John Chambers succinctly explains his way of thinking: "As leaders, if you don't reinvent yourself, change your organization structure; if you don't talk about speed of innovation, you're going to get disrupted."

Portraying such a responsive organization is quite opposite of what prevailed in the early twentieth century. At that time, the typical organization operated in a hierarchy where every decision was subject to constant challenge and re-examination. Organizations were slow and ponderous, and attempts at mobilizing corporate functions to react in a short timeframe would be an unreasonable expectation. There was hardly any semblance of "the harmony of his host."

Individuals during that period typically worked in their functional areas within large impersonal organizations that one critic described as "dreariness, not so much of physical deprivation but of a psychological void." Productivity was a major concern, and studies were continuously in progress to find approaches to increase efficiency and output.

The most famous of these research studies was conducted at the Hawthorne Works (a Western Electric factory) in Cicero, Illinois, from 1924 to 1932. Observers meticulously tracked results in worker productivity as changes were made in lighting, relocation of workstations, working hours, break times, and other areas.

Lighting, however, formed the basis of the study. In all instances where changes were made, productivity initially improved. When the observers completed their observations and left, productivity dropped to its previous levels.

Over the years, numerous organizational behavioral experts and industrial psychologists put forth unique and scholarly interpretations. The widely accepted view—known as the *Hawthorne effect*—is that the workers reacted positively in response to their awareness of being observed, rather than by any physical changes in their work space.

During that period, other researchers observed organizations, workers, and society through the written word. One of the more noteworthy books was William Whyte's *The Organization Man*, which suggested a degree of uniformity in the American middle class, reflected in standardized career paths, consumer tastes, sensibilities, and workplace obedience. Much of the writing about this group included David Riesman's *The Lonely Crowd* and C. Wright Mills' *White Collar Workers*. Each suggests that the rise of this working class was joyless.

How did the organization evolve from that early period to where it is today? What were the drivers that prompted business scholars and pragmatic business people to design the organization that is suitable for the digital environment?

To begin: The mere notion that management was a profession originated with the founding of business schools. The first was the Wharton School at the University of Pennsylvania, established in 1881. The central course of study at that time dealt with labor issues, preventing strikes, and maintaining discipline. The curriculum also dealt with handling great amounts of capital and other business processes.

It was not until 1908 that the Harvard Business School opened. At first, it promoted and taught science and engineering. Eventually the university opted for business, where the courses of study were influenced by the ideas of Frederick Taylor.

FREDERICK TAYLOR

Taylor claimed he had found a form of management that was "a true science, resting upon clearly defined laws." He based his method on the belief that for each task of an organization, there should be "one best way," found through careful analysis and measurement. Those who analyzed and measured, and acted upon the findings, would become part of a new profession.

Taylor distinguished between *planning* and *doing*. He thought that planning required very clever people, whereas with doing, it did not matter if people understood "the principles of this science." The more a worker could be treated as an unthinking machine the better, because without the complication of independent thought, it would be possible to calculate how best to extract optimal performance.

Part of what Taylor called *science* was the reliance on quantification and mathematics to establish the most efficient way to work. In turn, that approach called for "time-and-motion" studies with stopwatches to measure achievement, so that a rate could be set for its completion.

He also wrote in his bestselling book *The Principles of Scientific Management* that workers were natural "loafers" who failed to work as hard as they could. Without greater efficiency, he argued, management would have to reward workers with means other than pay—although he thought that pay was the best motivation of all.*

Even though labor unions rejected Taylor's concepts, overall his philosophy was in tune with the tempo of the times. He urged efficiency as a great national goal, rather than just an idea for companies. He hoped the principles would apply to all social activities from the management of homes to churches, universities, and government departments.

Efficiency, as he viewed it, fit well with the progressive connection that science, rather than intuition, could provide. He also felt his ideas worked

---

* Some of Taylor's theories are not unlike the ones contained in Douglas McGregor's well-known Theory X and Theory Y, which consist of two fundamental approaches to managing people. Theory X tends to use an authoritarian leadership style. In contrast, Theory Y leans toward a participative approach. Theory X is characterized by individuals' dislike for work. Though forced to work toward organizational objectives, they prefer to be directed. Above all, they want job security. With Theory Y, however, work is natural and enjoyable, it is self-directed to achieve organizational objectives, and individuals often seek greater responsibility.

as an objective basis for evaluating policies and reorganizing society to serve the needs of the majority rather than the self-interest of the few.

Considered "the father of scientific management,"—which was inscribed on his gravestone after he died in 1915—Taylor's followers included Henry Gantt and Frank and Lillian Gilbreth, who continued to develop and spread his ideas. They promoted a form of science, "aggressive rationality," which swept away custom and superstition for the benefit of management and labor. A group of theorists followed Frederick Taylor to form what became the Human Relations School.

THE HUMAN RELATIONS SCHOOL

As management theory evolved, the adherents to this school went beyond Taylor and stressed the importance of social networks in making organizations work. A key figure here was Elton Mayo, who gained fame as an interpreter of the Hawthorne experiments described above.

His research spoke directly to the core of executive concerns: how to calm the worker's irrational, agitation-prone mind; and how to develop and train managers and executives to do so. Mayo's underlying philosophy was deeply conservative, seeing conflict as a "social disease" to be remedied by a healthy cooperation across groups.

Others in the movement also had the idea of organizations as social systems, analogous to human bodies seeking some sort of equilibrium. To achieve equilibrium, the organization needed to achieve both efficiency and effectiveness. *Efficiency* means the ability to satisfy the individuals who make up the organization; *effectiveness* involves the ability to meet goals.

Therefore, management must formulate the organizational goals and decide how to meet them. But it must do so in a manner that keeps all members involved through every available form of direct and accessible communications. This notion, which now gets closer to today's organization, emphasized the importance of respect and cooperation, suggesting that collaboration was more important than material incentives and threats.

Along the same lines, and in addition to technical and social skills, managers needed to work actively to infuse the organization with appropriate values—which is now the cornerstone for developing a sound corporate culture. Otherwise, according to the theory, the organization would fail.

It was important "to educate and to propagandize" people to "inculcate" appropriate motives and perceptions. Consequently, executives must not only conform to a moral code but must also create moral codes for others, which would be reflected in high morale.

As the century progressed, the possibilities for maintaining a docile, regimented workforce receded with the growing strength of labor unions and the increasingly demanding nature of work requiring specialists. Moreover, while the original inspiration for the Human Relations School might have been to draw workers away from socialism and unions, it encouraged managers to recognize that their organizations were complex social structures rather than simple hierarchies, and that their workers would respond positively if treated as rounded human beings.

The approach risked replacing autocracy with paternalism as it struggled to work out how these developing views of organizational life would affect structures of power. The more these structures had to be addressed, and the more they had to be related to the wider social and economic changes underway, the more managers would need a strategy. What follows are the major influences in the evolution of the organization by the giants of industry.

GIANTS OF INDUSTRY

Of all the business leaders spanning several decades from the late 1800s through the 1940s, a few stand out who influenced the development of organizations and management. The primary ones include John D. Rockefeller, Henry Ford, and Alfred P. Sloan.

John D. Rockefeller

Ironically, Rockefeller's claim to fame cannot be used as a model for others to follow. He is best known for building an industry and developing Standard Oil into a virtual monopoly. As a leader, however, he had an exceptional ability to size up a market situation by seeing the full picture of its potential. Yet he could deal effectively with its individual components, such as sources of supply, distribution networks, government regulations, and competition. At times, however, his methods used a variety of questionable techniques.

By 1900, Standard Oil had reached the peak of its influence. The size of the international market, which already included significant competitors, meant that its relative position was bound to decline.

Rockefeller used skill, boldness, and power to overcome competition. Alliances and combinations, which were ingeniously developed as trusts, were used as a way of guaranteeing efficiency, stability, and, most importantly, control. However, he was already in a state of transition when forced to break up the trusts with the enactment of the Sherman Antitrust Act and the active intervention of then-US president Theodore Roosevelt.

Even where it looked as if Rockefeller was defeated, the opposite was the case. As the market expanded, it turned out that it was increasingly beyond the capacity of any single company to control a developing market of such size and complexity. The ability of smaller units to respond flexibly to new conditions eventually made for a stronger and more profitable industry, which was perpetuated by the likes of Henry Ford and Alfred P. Sloan.

Henry Ford

Ford framed an organization that linked to his strategic vision. He wished to "construct and market an automobile specially designed for everyday wear and tear," a machine to be admired for its "compactness, its simplicity, its safety, its all-around convenience, and its exceedingly reasonable price."

To accomplish this monumental task, he needed to get the price down to ensure the needed volume for a mass market—which did not exist at the time. That effort required new forms of manufacturing and assembly.

Thus, Ford's strategic thinking of a "universal car," built with high quality materials and simple to operate, resulted in the famous Model T. He then concentrated on manufacturing the one model in large numbers for, as it turned out, a longer period than warranted.

When asked by his salesmen for more models, Ford famously remarked: "Any customer can have a car painted any color that he wants so long as it is black." That said, the Model T was not to be a luxury item for a few, but one for "the great multitude."

To accomplish this feat, he installed the first assembly line in 1913. Tools and men were placed in sequence as each component moved along until the car was finished. This reduced the "necessity for thought on the part of the worker and his movements to a minimum." Ford claimed that his approach was a breakthrough not only in car manufacturing, but also in the development of the industrial society.

In effect, he gave a decisive impetus to two critical and related developments: the techniques of *mass production*, which in turn fed the goal of *mass consumption*. In his leadership approach, Ford sought personal control and oversight over what had become a massive company, with hundreds of thousands of employees and sales in the millions, yet he ran it "as if it were a mom-and-pop shop."

The company reached its peak in 1923 when it produced two million cars, including many tractors and trucks. By then, however, competition was developing from General Motors and Chrysler. While Ford stuck with the Model T, the others set the pace with a greater range of new cars.

By 1926, Ford's production was barely reaching 1.5 million vehicles and prices had dropped from $825 to $290. The rivals also began offering new forms of payment, such as accepting credit and installments. Ford was unwilling to offer similar inducements.

In the 1930s, almost submerged by competition, defeated by the unions, and suffering from a shameful reputation for anti-Semitism, Ford had little to offer the next generation of customers. The company's resurgence would have to wait to the beginning of World War II with the production of military vehicles, which would benefit from its vaunted assembly-line heritage. The industrial world was now ready for another type of leader.

Alfred P. Sloan

Sloan, president and later chairman of General Motors from 1923 through 1956, was responsible for shaping the modern corporation, as well as the automobile industry. His initial idea on becoming president depended on two propositions.

First, the company should be split up into divisions, each with its own chief executive with commensurate responsibility for all its operations. Second, specific organizational functions, absolutely necessary to the overall corporation's development, needed to be controlled at one level, notwithstanding that they might cause some contentious issues with division executives.

Sloan also had to face the reality that Ford in the early 1920s accounted for some 60% of all cars sold in the United States. To advance against such a formidable competitor, General Motors deployed its several divisions with ten models, from a basic car to a luxury vehicle.

The brilliance of this product-line strategy at that time is that these models did not reflect any existing generally accepted business concept. That is, before market segmentation became a popular strategy, Sloan's way of thinking represented a new way to view the market. It was about how different classes of customers might respond to variations in price and quality.

Consequently, the company could be organized to suit an evolving market. At that time, Sloan was not just relating to the market; he was actually reshaping it. The boldness of the strategy was not unlike Ford's initial approach to making a mass market. Sloan's approach to an organizational structure fit precisely with his strategy of marketing a full range of models under the slogan of a car "for every purse and purpose."

For instance, at the low end of the market, Sloan went up against the Model T with the company's Chevrolet model, but at a somewhat higher price than Ford's car. He astutely recognized that going head-to-head against Ford would be a wasteful strategy. Instead, he used as a decisive point the low end of the market by aiming for higher quality in order to justify a higher price.

Sloan's intention was to get sales from customers who were prepared to pay a bit more, but also to pick up sales from those at the next higher class who might prefer to pay a bit less. That maneuver would neutralize Ford by locking it in at the very low end of that segment.

And if Ford wanted to go upscale, it would confront Chevrolet, which was quickly solidifying its position. Within six years, General Motors led the market, selling 1.8 million vehicles in 1927. Clearly, Sloan demonstrated "a profound strategy coupled with far-reaching plans."

ORGANIZATIONAL THINKERS AND STRATEGISTS

A diverse range of thinkers contributed to organizational development. One of those individuals was an academic, Peter Drucker, who explored what it meant to manage a modern corporation. His book *The Concept of the Corporation* was the first to consider business as an organization and management as a specific organ doing specific kinds of work with specific responsibilities. He is credited with having established management as a discipline and the organization as a distinct entity. As such, they qualified as a discipline and a recognized field of study.

Drucker acknowledged Taylor's contributions but was skeptical of scientific management. He thought good results could be achieved by intuition and hunch. Further, Drucker blamed Taylor for separating planning from doing. Rather, he believed the job of management was "to make what is desirable first possible and then actual."

The essence of his philosophy was to alter circumstances by consciously directed actions. To manage a business was to "manage by objectives." To this end, he understood that whatever the long-term vision, it had to be translated into immediate and credible objectives when it came to implementation. (Look, again, at Part 3 for details on implementation.)

Drucker lucidly considered the complexities of both organizational structures and business environments. His numerous books set him up as the first contemporary management theorist. During his career, he became a consultant to leading companies, such as Ford, General Motors, and General Electric.

The Business–Military Connection

As noted in the Introduction, one specific group saw meaningful and pragmatic connections between military concepts and business applications, with specific applications to organizational development and business strategy.

Bruce Henderson of the Boston Consulting Group referenced the work of Sir Basil Liddell Hart. The eminent 20th-century British military historian gained fame for his *indirect approach*, which remains a valid strategy not only in its original usage in the military, but also as described in business planning (Part 3).

Henderson focused on the two fundamental principles devised by Liddell Hart, which were especially applicable for corporate executives and mid-level managers in competitive business situations.

First, direct approaches against a rival firmly in position almost never works and should never be attempted.* Second, to defeat an adversary, one must first upset its equilibrium, which is not accomplished by the main effort but must be done before the main effort can succeed.

Henderson especially valued Liddell Hart's emphasis on maneuvering through the indirect approach and concentrating strength against a rival's weaknesses. He also sensed the drama of competition and discussed the

---

* See previous example of Sloan's strategy of avoiding a head-to-head clash with Ford.

deception that might be employed to divert competitors. Strategy, he thought, could be applied to differences in leadership style, as well as to matters of overhead rate, distribution channels, or corporate image.

Also noted in the Introduction were the references to the military–business connection made by Professor Philip Kotler and by business strategists Jack Trout and Al Ries.

Another essential military reference worth incorporating here consists of the writings of Baron Antoine-Henri de Jomini (1779–1869.) As a general in the French and later in the Russian service, he was one of the most celebrated writers on the Napoleonic art of war. According to one historian, Jomini "deserves the dubious title of founder of modern strategy." His ideas were a staple at military academies.

Prior to the American Civil War, the translated writings of Jomini were the only works on military strategy that were taught at the United States Military Academy at West Point. His ideas shaped the basic military thinking of its graduates. It has been said that many a Civil War general went into battle with a sword in one hand and Jomini's *Summary of the Art of War* in the other.

Jomini's more famous maxims consist of the following, with others summarized in Table 32.1.

TABLE 32.1

Jomini's *Summary of the Art of War*

- In conflict an ally is to be desired, all other things being equal. Although a great organization will probably succeed over two weaker organizations, still the alliance is stronger than either would be separately.
- There are advantages in initiating conflict; there are also advantages in awaiting the rival upon one's own territory. Nevertheless, it is certain that an organization operating in its own territory is aided by an intimate knowledge of the territory, and the advantages of its numerous relationships.
- Under policy, we may include: the passions of the people to be fought, their systems, available reserves, financial resources; the connections and agreements they have; the character of their executives; the influence of internal groups on operation; the method of engaging in conflict; the geography and statistics of the territory to be attacked; and the resources and obstacles likely to be met.
- The organization should neglect nothing in obtaining a knowledge of these details; it is indispensable to take them into consideration in the development of all plans.
- The skill of a leader is one of the surest elements of victory.
- A good group commanded by a leader of ordinary capacity may accomplish great feats; a bad group with a good leader may do equally well; but a group will certainly do a great deal more if its own superiority and that of the leader is combined.

The leader should do everything to electrify his own people and to impart to them the same enthusiasm which he endeavors to repress in his adversaries.

A cherished cause and a leader who inspires confidence by previous success are powerful means of inspiring a group ... conducive to victory.

Enthusiasm propels the performance of great actions, but the difficulty is in maintaining it constantly; and when discouragement succeeds it, disorder easily results.

A leader ought to consider the intrinsic value of their people, as compared with the rival.

Concert in action makes strength; order produces this concert, and discipline insures order; and without discipline and order no success is possible.

By strategic movements, aim for the rival's decisive points.

A leader whose hands are tied by a council five hundred miles distant cannot be a match for one who has liberty of action, other things being equal.

ORGANIZATIONS: A PANORAMIC OVERVIEW

Continuing beyond the early days of the 20th century, what follows is a historical review by decade that highlights key events leading to today's digitally based organizations.

The 1950s

As Europe and Asia began rebuilding after the devastation of World War II, the 1950s became a period of overwhelming economic influence by the United States throughout most of the world. During that time, corporate planning dominated most of the larger US companies, which consisted primarily of production plans.

Such planning focused on satisfying an insatiable demand for consumer goods within the United States. It also aimed at supplying industrial products to help European and Asian countries ravaged by war to rebuild their economies and redevelop consumer markets.

At the highest organizational levels, executives developed long-term corporate plans, which also maintained a dominant financial focus. Rarely did lower-echelon managers participate in those planning sessions.

At the lower level, managers geared their planning to maximize productivity for the short-term satisfaction of market demand. Marketing as a distinct unifying function enveloping product development, marketing research, advertising, sales promotion, and field selling did not exist at that time.

The 1960s

Strong consumer demand for products characterized the 1960s. The business environment was marked by intensified economic growth in most of the industrialized countries. Yet serious competition still remained limited. And there was no urgency to change procedures, other than to keep the production lines moving efficiently. In general, what was produced was consumed.

In addition to developing markets among European industrialized countries, third-world countries slowly emerged as customers for products to sustain the basic needs of life. Such products included simple machines, some types of agricultural equipment, and basic transportation in the form of buses and bicycles.

Organizations began to look to business planning as a way to involve those executives who represented the core activities of manufacturing, research and development, sales, and distribution. As part of the longer-term strategy, there was a conscious effort to integrate diverse business functions through a coordinated plan of operations. In spite of this planning breakthrough, however, long-term plans were still kept separate from those short-term plans prepared by middle managers.

The 1970s

This decade triggered a transitional phase in planning and strategy. With the post-war rebuilding process about complete, its full effect was about to impact the world. European companies burst onto global markets. It was the Japanese companies, however, that generated the most aggressive and penetrating competition.

The full thrust of their competitive assault hit virtually every major industry from machine tools and consumer electronics to automobiles and steel. The new competitive situation ignited the surging movement to embrace market-based planning and competitive strategy.

In turn, marketing strategy signaled a period of market identification and expansion. In North America, customers demanded more varied products and services, and they were willing to pay for them. Responding to the continuing population shift out of the cities, businesses followed increasingly affluent customers into the expanding suburban shopping malls. In Western Europe and Asia, new markets continued to unfold, thereby increasing the consumption of consumer and industrial products.

Executives reshaped their organizations to reflect a customer-driven focus. They merged the individual plans of once-scattered activities, such as merchandising, advertising, sales promotion, publicity, and field selling, into a unified strategy to identify and satisfy changing market demands. Known as *marketing plans*, they were developed by middle managers and typically covered only a 1-year period.

Within those plans, managers emphasized emerging geographic markets, new technology applications, and international markets. They made extensive use of demographic profiles to define markets with greater precision. Beyond demographics, a new approach to market definition emerged that utilized *psychographics*, a profiling system that described prospects by life style and behavior.

Marketing as an independent business discipline expanded rapidly into undergraduate and graduate degree programs at universities worldwide. In keeping with the evolving and changing market conditions, a broad definition of marketing developed:

> *Marketing is a total system of interacting business activities designed to plan, price, promote, and distribute want-satisfying products or services to organizational and household users in a competitive environment at a profit.*

That definition emphasized satisfying customer needs and fulfilling the wants of different market segments. Further, a *total system of interacting business activities* called for integrating such functions as manufacturing, research and development, and distribution. In turn, the meaning called for the use of strategy teams consisting of individuals from each of those diverse functions. It reaffirmed that integrated business planning was underway.

By the late 1970s, still another form of planning took hold: *strategic planning*. Strategic planning built on the long-term, financially oriented corporate plans of the 1960s by adding a strategic focus to the process. More precisely:

> *Strategic planning is the managerial process of developing and maintaining a strategic fit between the organization and its changing market opportunities. It relies on developing:*
>
> - *A vision, mission, or strategic direction*
> - *Objectives and goals*
> - *Growth strategies*
> - *A business portfolio consisting of markets and products*

Corporations still used the generalized terms of *strategic planning*, *corporate planning*, or *business planning*. Regardless of the term used, the intent showed that volatile environmental, economic, industry, customer, and competitive factors required a more expansive and disciplined strategic thought process for effective planning and strategy development.

No longer would top-down, 1950s-style corporate planning driven by a production orientation suffice. The evolving competitive international marketplace of the 1970s required a more precise customer orientation satisfied by strategic planning and marketing planning.

The 1980s

The 1980s spurred the next stage of planning—strategic business planning—which merged two planning formats: the long-term strategic plan and the short-term marketing plan, as well as other operational plans.

There are several reasons why the strategic business plan evolved to this stage of the planning cycle:

1. While strategic planning permitted managers to create a long-term vision of how the organization could grow, for the most part it lacked implementation. A survey conducted by Deloitte & Touche

Consulting during this period indicated that while 97% of the Fortune 500 companies wrote strategic plans, only 15% of that elite group of companies ever implemented anything that came out of the plan.

2. Whereas business planning generally incorporated activities associated with the primary business functions, the planning period usually covered 1 year. Most importantly, no formal process linked the longer-term strategic plan that required an implementation phase to the shorter-term plan that warranted a strategic vision. That is, no unifying procedure satisfied the definition of "a total system of interacting activities designed to plan, price, promote, and distribute want-satisfying products to organizational and household users in a competitive environment."

Thus, the strategic business plan evolved to create a linkage of the strategic plan with the business plan. It connected the internal functions of the organization with the external and volatile changes of an increasingly competitive global environment. In turn, the plan became the primary mechanism for generating competitive strategies.

The 1990s

As corporations of the 1980s and 1990s re-engineered and downsized to create cost-effective, efficient, and lean organizations, a further innovation evolved. The middle-level manager was asked to develop a formal strategy plan for his or her product, service, or business unit.

Using the strategic business plan as a hands-on format, the manager could now conceptualize a product with a long-term strategic direction that focused on future customer and market needs. He or she could project what changes would take place in a framework of industry, consumer, competitive, and environmental areas, as well as how evolving technologies would impact the development of strategies. In addition, new groundbreaking software could identify changing buyer behavior and interpret the implications, so that business strategies could be further adjusted to achieve the plan's objectives.

The 2000s

With intensive worldwide competition from developed and developing countries on virtually every continent, and especially from China, organizations formed strategic alliances with major corporate mergers, as well as through specific joint efforts related to marketing, distribution, or product development.

Thus, the effective application of competitive strategies continued to saturate managers' time and energy as they immersed themselves in initiating efficient operations, outsourcing numerous functions, and adopting new technology innovations.

In particular, executives faced various types of competitive campaigns. Each had a distinctive purpose and required a customized action plan with objectives aligned to the strategic business plan's vision and the organization's culture. These appeared in various forms, as displayed by headline stories in the business press:

- "Wal-Mart Stores attacks one of the largest consumer-electronics chains, Best Buy Stores."
- "BMW shifts production to lightweight carbon fiber ahead of competitors to give its electric cars a performance advantage."
- "Google launches a new computer operating system and attacks Microsoft."
- "BASF challenges Monsanto's dominance in the global seed market."

Although the headlines may not have reached a crisis stage for those organizations under attack, they nevertheless did call for the defending firms to develop action plans.

Each of the above competitive situations, therefore, took on its own unique character. Companies began restructuring to respond rapidly with actions to gain an advantageous position, neutralize a competitor, or reverse declining sales. They used a variety of thrusts, such as introducing cutting-edge technologies, offering enhanced services, launching new products, initiating innovative delivery systems, or utilizing evolving social media.

THE AGE OF THE DIGITAL ORGANIZATION

The above historical review of how organizations evolved, the thought processes of the noteworthy leaders and writers of those times, and the strategies of the business giants over the decades have a finite connection with today's digital-age organization.

Some perceptive leaders see the linkages through the power of economic, environmental, technological, and behavioral influences that dictate organizational design, as did Rockefeller, Ford, and Sloan during their tenures. They shaped their organizations to suit strategic goals and the state of the market. Then, they combined, in various amounts, a customer-centric orientation with a production-centered focus.

As for the new workers, there is a firm linkage with the Human Relations School, which stressed the importance of social networks and the organization as a social system. Some industry observers portray increasingly large segments of the workforce as positive, creative, authentic, expressive, and spontaneous. Others describe them as independent, insubordinate, and less awed by the perceived wisdom of experts, their executives, or even the dictates of common sense.

With the emphasis now on data analytics, machine learning, and artificial intelligence as essential tools for competitive advantage, these talented workers are considered key differentiators in a digital world of competitive encounters. As such, they need to be nurtured and trained.

AT&T, for instance, delivered 50,000 big data–related training courses in one year, from 1-week boot camps to advanced PhD-level data science courses. As importantly, employees were taught to interact within an organizational structure that strives for collaboration among all corporate functions. That means influencing the two primary zones of activity that shape a dynamic marketplace.

First, make certain that the organization's products and services meet customers' needs. Second, strengthen the firm's ability to defend its markets against the inroad of aggressive competitors.

Both zones, in turn, contribute to a balanced organization that is agile enough to protect what was gained, yet maintains the internal capability to expand according to the objectives of its strategic business plan.

For the digital age, then, leadership is anchored to an organizational structure supported by stability, openness, resilience, and responsiveness. Above all, today's leaders must rely on their empowered staffs to embrace the vision and culture of the organization.

Appendix: Team Project Assessing Your Organization's Competitiveness

Carl von Clausewitz

Conflicts consist of a large number of engagements, great and small, simultaneous or consecutive. Each has a specific purpose relating to the whole.

(Therefore,) in conflict even the ultimate outcome is never to be regarded as final. The outcome is merely a transitory evil, for which a remedy may still be found in a variety of possible conditions at some later date.*

Clausewitz's pragmatic statement is anchored to the notion that giving into failure is not a viable option. He advises that "a remedy may still be found in a variety of possible conditions" to deal with a conflict.

However, searching for "possible conditions" is feasible only if the organization is in a state of readiness. And for any meaningful "remedy" to develop, your staff has to be fully aware of the company's capabilities, systems, and available resources.

To that end, the following assessment consists of 100 questions, which is divided into three areas:

1. Your firm's market environment.

2. Management procedures and policies. profound

3. Strategy factors.

---

* A portion of this insightful statement was also used in Chapters 17 and 32.

TEAM ACTIVITY

Answering the questions provide you and your team with a reliable review of your organization's competitiveness. Should you come across questions that don't apply to your business, modify them to fit your purpose, or leave them and move to the next section.

Depending on the size of your group, divide it into work teams of three or four individuals. Then reconvene the teams and have each present its findings. If there is major disagreement send the teams back for another round. When consensus is reached, take the information to the next step, which could mean giving assignments to individuals for further development or implementation.

Another option: Use the questions in open discussion with the entire group. Where appropriate you can invite a senior executive to observe or participate in the discussion. Or, you may choose to invite an outside consultant to act as a moderator.

PART I: REVIEWING OUR FIRM'S MARKET ENVIRONMENT

Consumers (End Users)

1. Who are our ultimate buyers?

2. What are the primary physical features and psychological issues that influence their buying decisions?

3. What key factors make up the demographic and psychographic (behavioral) profiles of our buyers?

4. When and where do they shop for and consume our products? With what frequency are purchases made?

5. What specialized needs do our products or services satisfy?

6. How well do they satisfy compared with similar offerings from competitors?

7. How can we segment our target markets with greater precision?

8. How do prospective buyers perceive our product in their minds? What research supports this viewpoint?

9. What are the economic conditions and expectations for our markets over the near and far term?

10. Are our consumers' attitudes, values, or habits changing? Is there reliable data available to track changes?

Customers (Intermediaries, Middlemen)

11. Who are our intermediate buyers? What is the extent of their influence throughout the supply chain?

12. How well do those intermediaries serve our target market?

13. How well do we serve their needs? What special services or assistance would solidify relationships?

14. What are the central issues that drive their buying decisions? Have there been any changes over the past 12 months? What are the projections for the next 12 months?

15. Has there been any significant movement in their locations relative to the end users?

16. What non-competing products do they carry? What competing product lines do they handle?

17. What percentage of total revenue does each competing product line represent compared with ours?

18. How much support do they give our product? What can be improved?

19. What factors made us select them and they select us?

20. How can we motivate them to work harder for us?

21. Do we need them?

22. Do they need us?

23. Do they use multiple channels, including e-commerce?

24. Would we be better off setting up our own distribution network?

25. Should we go direct to the end user? What are the advantages/disadvantages?

Competitors

26. Who are our competitors? What are their strengths and weaknesses?

27. Where are they located relative to our key customers?

28. How big are they overall, specifically within our product category? Where are they vulnerable?

29. What is their product mix? Are there any gaps in their mix that would create an opportunity for us?

30. Is their participation in the market growing or declining? What are the reasons in either situation?

31. Which competitors may be leaving the field? Why? What are the implications for us?

32. What new domestic competitors may be entering the market? What market niches are they filling? Or what comparative advantage are they using?

33. What new foreign competitors may be on the horizon? How threatening are they?

34. Which strategies and tactics appear particularly successful or unsuccessful when used by competitors?

35. What new directions or use of technologies, if any, are competitors pursuing? Which of their strategies are successful in such areas as: selecting market niches, products, pricing, distribution, or others.

Other Relevant Environmental Components

36. What legal and environmental constraints affect our competitiveness? What are the immediate and long-term concerns?

37. To what extent do government regulations restrict our flexibility in making market-related decisions?

38. What do we have to do to comply with regulations?

39. What political or legal developments are looming that will improve or worsen our situation?

40. What threats or opportunities do advances in technology hold for our company, such as artificial intelligence and machine leaning?

41. How well do we keep up with technology in day-to-day operations? How do we rank in the industry and against key competitors?

42. What broad cultural shifts are occurring in segments of our market that may impact our business?

43. What consequences will behavioral, demographic, and geographic shifts have for our business?

44. Are any changes in resource availability foreseeable, e.g., finances, equipment, personnel, raw materials, or suppliers?

45. How do we propose to cope with environmental, social, or human rights issues that could impact our business?

PART II: REVIEWING OUR MANAGEMENT PRACTICES AND POLICIES

Analysis

46. Do we have an internal market research function, or do we rely primarily on outside resources? To what extent do staff and outside agents participate in obtaining competitive intelligence?

47. Do we systematically use competitor intelligence to develop plans and strategies? Is it applicable for going on the offensive to expand into new markets, as well as for defending existing positions?

48. Do we subscribe to any data services?

49. Before we introduce a new product or service do we test its acceptance among customers, as well as consider how to position it against competitors?

50. Do what extent are market-related decisions based on formal market research, as well as informal feedback from field personnel?

Planning

51. Do we have a formalized procedure to develop a strategic business plan?

52. To what extent do we seek input from empowered individuals in other areas of the organization?

53. Do our long- and short-term objectives complement our company's vision?

54. What procedures do we use to locate gaps in customers' needs?

55. Do we develop clearly stated short-term and long-term objectives? How are they prioritized to avoid internal conflicts with other business units?

56. Are our objectives realistic, achievable, and measurable?

57. Do we utilize appropriate metrics to assess performance and make essential mid-course corrections?

58. How effective are we in integrating what-if scenarios into our plan and thereby be prepared with "a remedy" to react rapidly to competitive threats?

59. Are our core strategies and tactics for achieving our objectives aligned with our corporate culture?

60. Is there a systematic screening process in place to identify opportunities and threats, such as a SWOT (strengths, weaknesses, opportunities, threats) analysis or similar approach?

61. How aggressively are we considering diversification or joint ventures as it relates to planning for growth?

62. How effectively are we segmenting markets to determine decisive points?

63. Are we committing sufficient resources to accomplish our objectives?

64. Are our resources optimally allocated to the major elements of our business?

65. How well do we tie-in our plans with the other functional plans of our organization?

66. Is our plan realistically followed or just filed away?

67. Do we continuously monitor environmental movements to determine the viability of our plan?

68. Do we have a centralized activity to collect and disseminate market and competitor intelligence?

69. Do we have an individual who oversees the sharing of technology and communicating market data among business groups?

Organization

70. Does our firm have a high-level function to analyze, plan, and oversee the implementation of our strategic efforts?

71. How capable, dedicated, and empowered are our personnel?

72. Is there a need for more skills and leadership training?

73. Are leadership responsibilities structured to best support the needs of different products, target markets, and sales territories?

74. Does our organization's culture embrace and practice the market-driven, customer-first concept?

PART III: REVIEWING STRATEGY FACTORS

Product Policy

75. What is the makeup of our product mix?

76. How effective are our new product development plans?

77. Does it have optimal breadth and depth to maintain customer loyalty and prevent unwelcome entry by aggressive competitors?

78. Should any of our products be phased out?

79. Do we carefully evaluate any negative ripple effects on the remaining product mix before we decide to phase-out a product?

80. Have we considered modification, repositioning, and/or extension of mature products?

81. Do any of our products lend themselves to a branding strategy?

82. What immediate additions, if any, should be made to our product mix to maintain a competitive edge?

83. Which products are we best equipped to make ourselves and which items should we outsource and resell under our own name?

84. Do we routinely check product safety and product liability?

85. Do we have a formalized and tested product recall procedure? Is it effective?

Pricing

86. How effective are our pricing strategies? To what extent are our prices based on cost, demand, market, or competitive considerations?

87. How would our customers likely react to higher prices? What losses can we expect, if any?

88. Do we use temporary price promotions and, if so, how effective are they?

89. Do we suggest resale prices within the supply chain?

90. How do our wholesale or retail margins and discounts compare with those of the competition?

Marketing/Communications

91. Do we state our communications objectives clearly?

92. Do we spend enough, too much, or too little on marketing?

93. Are our communication themes effective?

94. Is our media mix adjusted to the optimal use of the Internet and social media?

95. Do we make aggressive use of the media to stimulate sales and disrupt competitive actions?

Personal Selling and Supply Chain

96. Is our salesforce (if any) at the right strength to accomplish our objectives and to what extent will the Internet affect salesforce activities?

97. Is it optimally organized to provide market coverage; and to meet customers' logistical, technical, and service needs?

98. Is it adequately trained and motivated as compared with key competitors?

99. Have we enhanced our supply chain, or are there opportunities for improved performance?

100. How do our field personnel rank against our major competitors?

In sum, the above assessment is highly useful in broadening your group's perspective to think like strategists. It should clarify their thinking and permit them to "find a remedy...in a variety of possible conditions."

Therefore, use these questions as general guidelines and customize them to suit your specific needs.

Index